Great Words of the Christian Faith

Great Words of the Christian Faith

DONALD COGGAN
Archbishop of Canterbury

Nashville • Abingdon

GREAT WORDS OF THE CHRISTIAN FAITH

Copyright © 1978 by Abingdon

Library of Congress Cataloging in Publication Data

COGGAN, FREDERICK DONALD,1909-
Great words of the Christian faith.
1. Christian life—Anglican authors. I. Title.
BV4501.2.C632   248'.48'3   78-9801

ISBN 0-687-15730-7

Scripture quotations noted NEB are from the New
English Bible, copyright © the Delegates of the
Oxford University Press and the Syndics of the
Cambridge University Press, 1961, 1970.

Poetry on page 69 is from "Peace and Joy" by G. A.
Studdert-Kennedy. Copyright 1924 by Harper &
Brothers. Reprinted by permission of Hodder &
Stoughton, Ltd., publishers.

Lines on pages 92 are an extract of two stanzas from a
hymn by Robert Bridges (1844–1930), after Joachim
Neander (1650–80), from the *Yattendon Hymnal.*
Used by permission of Oxford University Press.

MANUFACTURED BY THE PARTHENON PRESS AT
NASHVILLE, TENNESSEE, UNITED STATES OF AMERICA

For Jean
Dear wife and fellow worker
in Jesus Christ

Preface

It is an honor to introduce you to this book. These words were written for and were first presented as sermons on the Episcopal Series of the Protestant Hour, produced by the Episcopal Radio-TV Foundation of Atlanta, Georgia. They are presented now in book form so that you may "read, mark, learn and inwardly digest" the rich material.

Many people in our churches today are theologically illiterate. Yet, they yearn for meaning in their lives. They want to plumb the depths of their Judeo-Christian heritage, their religious roots. They want to respond to life in the light of that heritage. They want to understand eternal truths in a way that a twentieth-century person can comprehend them and live them.

In this book, Archbishop Coggan presents these eternal truths with clarity and insight. He makes the old new. His simple words reflect his own depth of faith. He teaches us the Christian faith as he wears his high office—with grace and humility.

The 101st Archbishop of Canterbury wears a simple pectoral cross on which is inscribed in Latin, "Woe unto me if I preach not the gospel" (I Corinthians 9:16). Through this book, F. Donald Coggan preaches the gospel of Jesus Christ.

We commend *Great Words of the Christian Faith* to you in your pilgrimage to know the faith, to practice the faith, and to share that faith.

Harold Barrett Robinson
Bishop of Western New York
Chairman, Episcopal Radio-TV Foundation

Contents

Great Words of the Christian Faith

1. Humanity

What is Man? A variety of answers is available. The chemist could reply: "I am a bunch of chemicals worth a few coins." The materialist could reply: "I am a bunch of desires crying out for satisfaction." The anthropologist could reply: "I am the highest in the long series of the animal creation." All of these answers would be true, but all would be quite inadequate. They do not satisfy the thinking person. They leave too many questions unanswered.

There are things about "me" which call for deeper answers than these. Within me are mysterious factors which cannot be left out of consideration. I can *relate* to others. I can *love*—in a way which animals can*not*. I find myself compelled to ask questions: e.g., What happens when I die? Do I snuff out like a candle which has fulfilled its function and is now at an end? Or is there a beyond, into which I am destined to enter? I have the ability to *appreciate*—in a way which, so far as I can tell, animals can*not*: I can respond to beauty—in art, architecture, literature, music; I can respond to truth and to goodness; I can respond to *God*—if I cannot, I belong to a species which can, millions and millions of whom have so responded and do so respond: they *worship*. I am a creature with worship potential.

I realize, of course, that there are those who hardly ever ask these questions. They have become so absorbed with—so obsessed by—the material things around them that, when such questions raise their heads, they crush them. "Let us eat and drink, for tomorrow we die." That is about the only philosophy to which they will give heed. The thorns have squeezed the life out of the young plant. Materialism, and the pursuit of pleasure, have won the day.

I doubt whether you would be reading these words if you were like that. You want to think, and perhaps to decide, about these great issues.

What has the Christian faith to say about this question: *Who am I?* The Bible has a wide variety of answers. Man's transitoriness, the fact of his mortality and fragility, is expressed by some writers who say "he is a breath." That is to say he is like a puff of wind, here for a moment and then gone! "His breath is in his nostrils"— deprive him of that and he is no more! Other writers speak of persons as being "like the beasts that perish"—a few years of activity and productivity, and death and burial follow. That's that!

That is all true, so far as it goes. These are glimpses of the obvious, and they don't go far. They come largely from a period when the Jews had little notion, if any, of an afterlife. But there are other answers which take us further, even in the Old Testament. One of the psalmists went out of his tent one night and looked up into the sky. He knew nothing of what we now know of the galaxies, of outer space, of millions and millions of light-years. But as he looked up, something of the mystery and immensity of the universe struck him. He found himself praying: "When I consider thy heavens, the work of thy fingers, the moon and the stars, which thou hast ordained; what is man that thou art mindful of him? and the son of man, that thou visitest him?" Well, what answer would you expect him to have given? Man is like a breath, like one of the beasts that perish, a poor little creature of short life-span and negligible significance! But that is precisely what he did *not* say. Listen as he continues his prayer to God: "Thou hast made him little lower than the angels" ("little less than a god," as the New English Bible has it), "and hast crowned him with glory and honor." A breath, a beast—that won't do for an answer. The psalmist refuses to be threatened by a sort of astronomical intimidation—size, even the size of the universe, is not what finally counts. He, the psalmist standing outside his Eastern tent, *knows* that the stars are there. It is scarcely conceivable that *they* know that *he* is there! But he goes on with his prayer, his argument, his colloquy: "Thou madest him to have dominion over the works of thy hands; thou hast put all things under his feet, all sheep and oxen, yea, and the beasts of the field; the fowl of the air, and the fish of the sea." Man in fact is a creature vested with divine authority—himself responsible, answerable, to God for the use he makes of the material world, God's agent. He is not a machine, he is not an automaton. He is responsible for the physical world around him, for the use he makes of nature. In that responsibility, the fact of his being *answerable* to God, lies his uniqueness. This it is above all else which separates him off from the other members of the animal creation—he is responsible for nature, for others, for himself.

Is that the meaning—or, rather, a tiny part of the meaning—of the phrase in one of the Genesis stories of creation which says that man is "made in the *image* of God"? There is that in him which can answer to God—like answering to like; and only when he answers in adoration and worship does he reach the full stature of his humanity. Is that the meaning of my being made in the image of God? Indeed it is not the total meaning, but a large and important part of it.

Men and women are made *for God*. But we cannot leave it at that. We are made *for community living*. Those old Genesis stories— what profound truths they hold! To say they are not scientific, or historical in the sense that Adam and Eve were historical figures just as Julius Caesar and Bonaparte were, and therefore that we need give no heed to them, is to engage in an act of great folly. If we were to do that, we should be throwing the baby out with the bath water. These stories were not written to teach us science—we go elsewhere for *that* kind of knowledge. They *were* written to teach us about the nature of God and man and human destiny—the things that finally matter. And that they do with extraordinary perception. So in the Genesis stories of creation we are told that when God had created man he saw his need for companionship and provided Adam with his Eve. "It is not good that man should live alone." No indeed: he is made for community—for the love that comes from others and that he himself can give to others; for the rough and tumble of community living, whereby his corners can be knocked off and his character made. Hence the basic importance of family life, and living membership of the church, the family of God.

We must go further, and assert that we are made *for eternity*. The study of man's life on this planet makes it abundantly clear that there is within him an incorrigible longing to know what lies beyond this little life. Nor is it only curiosity which makes him want to peer over the wall of his finitude. There is in him a sense of right and wrong, of sheer justice. It is quite clear that in this world justice is by no means always done—the goodies do not always get away with it, nor are the baddies always punished. The philosophy of the psalmist that the man who takes God as his refuge will be delivered from the snare of the fowler and from the deadly pestilence—that the Christian pilot will come home safe and the Christian child escape disease (to modernize the language)—is just too facile. What then? Must there not be a life beyond? Or do Hitler and Mother Theresa have the same destiny? This is by no means the total argument for an afterlife or, if you will, for heaven and hell. But it is part of it. Don't try to silence those questions about the afterlife, about eternity, which keep poking up their heads. They are part of your manhood, of your womanhood. Man is made for eternity.

Let us recapitulate. We are made for God, made for community, made for eternity. Yes, and made for *service.* The "proper Man," as Martin Luther called Jesus, said that he "did not come to be served, but to serve, and to give up his life as a ransom for many" (NEB). John tells us that Jesus said: "To this end was I born, and for this cause came I into the world, that I should bear witness unto truth." Born to serve; born to bear witness to truth. Born, in fact, for the service of truth, and so for the service of humanity. This was the program of the "proper Man." And we lesser mortals reach our fulfillment, and find our consummate joy, only when that sort of program becomes our passion. The Indian poet Tagore put it well. He wrote:

I slept and I dreamt that life was all joy;
I awoke and saw that life was but service;
I served and understood that service was joy.

Who am I? What is man? A bunch of chemicals? A bundle of desires? The last and highest in the animal series? It looks as if I am much more than any of these, or all of these put together. Paul puts it in words of incomparable grandeur: "God," he said, "knew his own before ever they were, and also ordained that they should be shaped to the likeness of his Son" (NEB) There is man's destiny. There is *my* destiny in the plan of God—to "be shaped to the likeness" of Jesus. "Shaped"—the word makes one think of a potter at his work, or of a carpenter hammering away until the picture in his mind becomes a reality in his hands. God the great Potter has a pattern in his mind, a character he wants to shape and to form. He wants me to be like Jesus.

The process begins in the here and now. But it does not end with the dissolution of my body. "Here and now," wrote John, "we are God's children; what we shall be has not yet been disclosed, but we know that when it is disclosed we shall be like him, because we shall see him as he is" (NEB).

That is a mighty expectation—with direct effect on conduct. "Everyone who has this hope before him purifies himself as Christ is pure" (NEB).

2. God

Let us begin by facing the fact that we cannot expect to find neat and tidy answers or clear and totally satisfying definitions or descriptions. God is infinitely greater than we are, or he would not *be* God. All theology—God-talk, as the word literally means—runs out into mystery. While we try to understand, and while we bring our best brains to bear on the subject, we shall always reach a point where sight is blinded and where faith, wonder, and adoration alone can operate. Wonder is next door to worship, and there, frequently, we must rest.

From the days of prehistory, people have been asking questions about God or about the gods. Very early in the history of our race man was conscious of a power beyond himself, outside himself. Very often he responded in fear—the wind and the fire, mysterious elements in his little universe, were terrifying factors. The strange powers of *life* which he found in his own body; the power of procreation which he only dimly understood; the power of growth in nature which he saw at work in plants, trees, and crops; the disasters caused by too much sun or too little water, by flood and pestilence and fire—these things seemed out-side of his control. Could it be that there was a god, or that there were gods, who at times were beneficent and at other times destructive? Was it—were they—totally capricious? Or were *their* actions somehow linked to *his?* Did they visit him in kindness or in vengeance? What were the gods like? Could you even begin to posit the question in terms of personality and ask it as we are asking it today: *Who* is God? Should you think in terms of a pantheon—a gallery of gods—or would it be better to think of one God, alone, supreme over heaven and earth? And if so, what was he like?

Ancient literature is full of such questions. It is full, too, of men's attempts at answers. Human sacrifice, animal sacrifice, aimed at the propitia-tion of angry deities or the expiation of man's sins and follies, bestrew the literature of the ages. Archaeologists have dug up the evidence, in many parts of the world, for all of us to see.

Now what has the Christian faith to say about this central and crucial question?

The Bible gives us abundant evidence of the central place which this question occupied in the thinking, the puzzling, of men as they begat their families, grew their crops, buried their dead. The Old Testament reeks with the stench of endless animal sacrifices. And *then* questions began to be asked. Was this really the kind of sacrifice that God wanted, the kind that pleased him most? Suppose it were offered by men whose hands were stained with *human* blood, or whose practices were corrupt, or who, to their own selfish profit, were grinding down the poor? Would *this* be acceptable to God? Was it possible that the sacrifice that God liked was the sacrifice of a broken and contrite heart? Was *this* what pleased him? Was all the paraphernalia of altars and animals and priests and blood unnecessary? Was ethical conduct more important than ritual correctness?

If you read the Psalms, you can hear, in certain of them, these questions being asked. But it is especially when you come to the writings of the prophets of Israel who lived in the eighth century before Christ that there begins to emerge, with a clarity unknown before, the picture of a God, one God and only one, who must be thought of primarily in terms of justice and of love. Read, for example, the book of Amos or the opening chapters of Isaiah, and there you will see depicted a God who *minds* how his worshipers live. What is their relationship with their employees—is it fair and aboveboard? Or is it one of oppression, of grinding the faces of the poor? These writers pour scorn on those who, as we should say, go to church and do everything correctly there while at the same time their actions are unjust and unethical. Very clearly, disconcertingly clearly, there stands out from the pages of these prophets the picture of a God who is essentially and totally a God of *justice.*

The prophet Hosea gives us a different picture of God—one not inconsistent with that of Amos and Isaiah but with an emphasis deeper and more tender than theirs. His accent is on the *love* of God. He is not alone among the writers of the Old Testament in stressing this aspect of the character of God. The psalmist spoke of it: "Like as a father pitieth his children, so the Lord pitieth them that fear him." "Have we not all one Father? Did not one God create us?" another prophet, Malachi, asks. Yes, to them God was a God of fatherly love and care. But Hosea's concept sprang from the wells of his own experience of unrequited love, of love thrown back in his face by the one he had loved and loved still. His wife, Gomer, had run off with another man, and Hosea was left heartbroken. In just such fashion, God's people, his nation of Israel, had—yes, Hosea uses the vivid imagery —committed adultery against God and run away "a-whoring" after other gods, stupid, powerless, futile though they were. And yet, God loved them still. As Hosea, brokenhearted, was ready to receive Gomer back if she would but repent and come, so God, the broken-hearted God, was ready to take back into the arms of his compassion the people who had defected from him. God, so Hosea insists, is essentially a God of *love.*

Here in the insights of the prophets is, I be-lieve, a revelation—I use the word advisedly —a revelation of the character of God, a God of justice and love, not vouchsafed to other nations—to the Greeks or Romans or any others—in anything approaching the depth or clarity which the Old Testament writers show. Here is the beginning of a deeply satisfying answer to our question: Who is God?

"The beginning," I said. Yes, the beginning. Or, we could equally well say, the *basis*. For it was on this basis that Jesus built when he taught about God.

He taught about him in two main ways, using two main pictures, if you will (for we can only think of God in picture or metaphorical language, simply because we are thus limited by being only human).

First, he spoke of God as *King*. "The kingdom of God" was apparently the main theme of his teaching work—the reign, the domination of God over his willing subjects. Now, any king worthy of the title must be a king who governs in justice (here are our friends Amos and Isaiah again!) and who, just because he does that, has the right to look for a response of obedience on the part of his subjects. In a very remarkable way the reign of God had begun to operate with the coming of Jesus himself. Around him were beginning to gather a group of men and women who were willing, for all their failures, to acknowledge his domination over their lives. The day when God's total domination would be universally acknowledged was obviously still future. But a toehold on the territory which was rightly his had been made, and victory was assured!

Secondly, he spoke of God as *Father*. Here again, Jesus based his teaching on that of the Old Testament, but he developed it in a unique way. He spoke of a Father who did not give up his children when they ran away from him and acted the fool. Rather, he waited for them, ran to meet them, flung his arms around them, and received them back. He was like a shepherd who had an ache in his heart until the hundredth sheep was back, with the ninety-nine, in the fold. He would search until he found.

But this teaching of Jesus about the kingly justice of God and the fatherly love of God was no mere theory. There is nothing of the cold lecture room about the teaching of Jesus. It sprang from his own experience of God. If God was King, then Jesus would show him complete obedience—"not my will, but thine be done." If God was Father, then Jesus would return to him the response of total love. In the light of that response of obedience and love his life was lived, even to the death on the Cross. And *that* was to be the way for his followers.

It is when men fail to respond in this way that they run, as individuals and as communities, into desperate trouble. "The sin of the world," the sin that taints every one of us in lesser or greater degree, is the refusal to respond to God as King and Father. If I put self first, where I should put him first—if I run away from the love which is always going out to me from the Father's heart—then I get entangled in "the sin of the world." And who of us has not done just that? Not one. We are all sinners in need of the gracious forgiving of our Father—God.

3. Jesus

Here is a name which has tantalized and haunted men and women for nineteen and a half centuries. That it does so still today can be seen in the titles of musicals such as *Jesus Christ Superstar,* as well as in the growth and activities of such groups as the Jesus People. We may criticize the musicals for the presentations which they make of the central figure. We may condemn the Jesus People, if so we will, for the inadequacy of the Jesus they admire. But the fact remains that he fascinates them, he haunts them, he arouses wonder in them. So it is—and has been for long years—with the writers of lives of Jesus. Some have obviously gone grievously wrong. Others have told us more about the writers themselves than they have about the One of whom they are supposed to be writing. Some stick close to the biblical texts. Others emphasize one facet of the gospel picture to such a neglect of other facets that we are left with little more than a caricature. But, I repeat, the fascination, the lure, is *there.* He provokes, as none other has done.

Who *is* Jesus? Let us begin with the known (though, be it added, with what has not been totally explored, nor is ever likely to be). He is a *teacher.* A superb teacher, most would add. The supreme Teacher, many would assert. "Never man spake like this Man," many would claim, using words first uttered by his contemporaries.

The point scarcely needs elaborating. If it is the mark of a great teacher to be able to speak with simplicity of the profound, then Jesus, if we may say so with reverence, must be awarded top marks. In fact, the parables of Jesus are deceptively simple, if by "deceptive" we mean that they *could* lead us to think that on a first reading we have seen all that there is to them. The very reverse is the case. Rather, they are like diamonds. Turn the stone one way, and it flashes red; another, and it flashes green; another, and you see blue. The parables are provocative—of thought, ideas, action. Any one reader may see a variety of interpretations. And there can be almost as many interpretations as there are interpreters. The parables are not a closure to further thought. They are a stimulus to thought, and not only to thought but to action. Jesus used the imagination as a road to the will.

If you want to see the eternal put to you in terms of the temporal, of the everyday, then go to the parables. Only beware, if you tend to be lazy! Jesus had a way of prefacing his parables with a question like this: What do you think? How does this appeal to *you?* He throws the ball into our court, and he will never let you get away with ready-made answers.

Then from this assertion about Jesus as a supreme—*the* supreme—Teacher, we could go on to assert—and we should carry multitudes with us in the assertion—that he is our *Example.* This is an authentic New Testament emphasis, though the specific references are comparatively few. The clearest, perhaps, is that in which the writer of the First Letter of Peter, speaking about suffering and how it is to be dealt with, points to Christ: "Christ suffered on your behalf, and thereby left you an example; it is for you to follow in his steps" (NEB). The abused did not retort with abuse, the sufferer uttered no threats, and so on. A similar argument is used by Paul, at least in some translations of the passage in the Letter to the Philippians (2:5-8): "Let your bearing towards one another arise out of your life in Christ Jesus. . . . [He] made himself nothing, . . . He humbled himself. . . . [He] accepted even death—death on a cross" (NEB).

This appeal to Jesus as our example has been a strong stimulus to heroic discipleship on the part of many of his followers down the centuries—and still is. As they meditate on his character, and particularly on his passion, the image on the screen of their mind is more than the recollection of a good man who lived long ago. It merges into their experience of a living Lord, who by his Spirit makes possible the realization in their own characters of at least something of what they have glimpsed in Jesus their example.

But let us be honest about this: Jesus seen simply as a great teacher or a wonderful example would *by itself* be a concept liable to lead us to despair. I have great sympathy with the deformed boy who burst into tears as he looked at the glorious figure of the Belvedere Apollo, so perfect in every limb. "I can never be like that! I can never be like that," he sobbed. An example of perfection is by itself powerless.

Is this all, then, that we can say about Jesus—that he was a great teacher and is a great example? *By no means*—certainly not if we are to be true to the witness borne by the writers of the New Testament. Now here we come to a phenomenon which calls for careful and honest thinking. It is astounding to find that only some twenty years or so after the death of Jesus, Christians were claiming that he was the One through whom all things were made. "For us", Paul wrote, "there is one God, the Father, from whom all being comes, towards whom we move; and there is one Lord, Jesus Christ, through whom all things came to be, and we through him" (I Cor. 8:6 NEB). John, later in the century, was to work that out in more detail in the passage which is read as the Christmas Gospel (John 1:1-14). But here was Paul, Jewish monotheist that he was, outlining the fact that God's agent in redemption was also his agent in creation. So Paul's letters begin with greetings from God the Father and the Lord Jesus Christ, as if God's throne were a shared throne. It is of a piece with John's tremendous assertion that *Jesus was the Word of God.* He did not merely *convey* the word of God, as the prophets had done before him. He *was* the Word of God.

What is a word? It is a miraculous thing, when you come to think of it. It is a means by which there is conveyed from me to you something which is in my mind or on my heart. So, when John says that "when all things began, the Word already was. The Word dwelt with God, and what God was, the Word was" (NEB), and when he goes on to identify that Word with Jesus of Nazareth and to say that that "Word became flesh" and "came to dwell among us," he is making a stupendous assertion. He is saying: "If you want to know what is in the mind of the Eternal, what the heart of the Eternal is like, what the will of the Eternal is, you will find it, revealed, in the word, in Jesus of Bethlehem, of Nazareth, crucified and risen."

When God was incarnate in the Person of Jesus, it was not as if some visitor from Mars landed on our planet. The Word made flesh came *to his own,* to the universe that owed its existence to him; and those who had come into being by his creative activity received him not.

Here is mystery—did I not warn you that all great theology, all God-talk, runs out into mystery? It cannot be otherwise, and we should not seek to have it otherwise. Of course we must use human categories of speech; being human, we cannot do otherwise. We know in part. We speak with all the limitations of human language and thought. If that is what we mean by *myth,* then so be it; mythologically we must speak. When we refer to Jesus as the "Son of God," we do not infer that God, who is Spirit and not flesh, "begat" Jesus as a human father begets a son or daughter. What we do mean is that, in a unique way, this Jesus reflects the Being, and conveys the Mind, of him who sent him. We mean that in him, as in no one else, we see the effulgence of God's splendor and the stamp of God's very being. In him who created the universe and sustains it by his word, we see God's creative activity and his redemptive power at work. Here in Jesus is the power of God and the wisdom of God. Here is displayed, as nowhere else, that intervention in the affairs of men which, if responded to, leads to their salvation, their deliverance from all that spoils their development and limits their growth.

Jesus is not only teacher and example. He is the Word of God, the Son of God, the Savior.

No wonder that the early Christians used to have a fish as one of their favorite Christian symbols. In Greek the word for fish is *ichthus;* its letters are the initial letters of the words "Jesus Christ Son of God Savior." It was a meaningful symbol to those who had found life in his person.

I cannot leave our question, Who is Jesus?

without referring to one other word which the first Christians loved to use in describing him—an example followed by their successors up to and including the present day. They loved to call him *Lord.*

Now, the word they used for Lord was a very elastic one. It was used as a title of God in the Old Testament very frequently. But it was also used in the world to which Jesus came and in which Christianity was born just as we should use the word "Sir." If you go to Greece today, and in a restaurant call a waiter to bring you a drink, he will use this word when he says "Yes, sir" to your call. So it can be used very widely. How was it used in the New Testament in relation to Jesus? In a wide variety of ways. When the apostles used it (or its Aramaic equivalent) in conversation with Jesus, I suppose they used it much the same way as my students used to call me "sir" when I was teaching them. But in many passages it meant much more than that. It was shorthand to express a relationship of a most meaningful kind. Often it had overtones of deity about it. Always it conveyed the idea of one who exercised domination over them, a domination which they rejoiced to acknowledge and in which they found their complete freedom. What a paradox that was! But in the heart of that paradox, in their willing obedience and total abandonment to him whom they called Lord, they found their life. And that life was of such a kind that they called it eternal life—by which they meant not merely that it was everlasting, but that it was of such a quality that all other life was mere existence.

Our question was, Who *is* Jesus? Somehow we could not say, Who *was* Jesus? for that would be patently wrong. For the first Christians he was a present, living reality. They did not look back nostalgically to a dead Christ, as we might look back to bygone history and say, "If only we had Churchill, or Roosevelt, present with us, things would be different." They *had* Jesus present with them, and things *were* different because of his living presence.

> Nearer was He than breathing;
> Closer than hands or feet.

"Though now ye see him not, yet believing, ye rejoice with joy unspeakable and full of glory."

No, they did not just look *back.* They looked up, to where he reigned; and *around,* to where he was at work.

They did.

We do, who love his name, the name of Jesus which is above every name.

4. Church

It is a common experience today to hear people say something like this: "I like Jesus. But I don't like the church. I like the simple teaching of Jesus, but the church seems to me to be a kind of complicated addition that people thought up after his time. A pity they didn't leave things as they were. Give me the Sermon on the Mount."

If those who talk this way knew their facts better than they generally do, they could add this to their argument—that the word "church" only occurs twice in all the four Gospels—so there!

But it's not so simple as that! Far from it. Let's begin at the beginning.

In the old Genesis picture story of man's beginning—and it *is* a picture story with a profound meaning to it—you may recall that when God had created man he said that it was not right for man to be alone. So he was joined by woman, and family life began. This is a picture-story way of saying that, if the species is to continue and if people are to develop fully, they must do it in community. We must learn how to live in a family, else we will be warped and wizened. So the family became a community from which God chose a nation, the main purpose of whose existence was to show men and women what he was like. That the nation failed him and that the faithful were reduced to only a remnant is neither here nor there for our present purposes. The point is that in the mind of God his revelation of himself was to be incorporated in and transmitted through a body of people. For God's glory and for their good there must be a community.

After the death and resurrection of Jesus, the little community which had gathered round him during his ministry and had scattered in fear at the time of his death gathered together again— except for poor Judas, who had committed suicide. Renewed and empowered by the Holy Spirit at Pentecost, they grew rapidly. Saul of Tarsus, that stormy petrel, was converted and joined them. Little groups sprang up, mushroom-like, all over the Mediterranean world. They met in one another's homes (before bigger buildings had to be provided for their increasing numbers). They broke bread and poured out wine and partook of both, as their Lord had commanded them. They listened to the Scriptures of the Old Testament and to letters which people like Paul were writing and which were circulating, and to words of explanation and exhortation which various people among them or visitors to them felt they must deliver. They found that in the fellowship of sacrament and prayer and interchange of experience there was a strength which could be found nowhere else. It was not right that any Christian should be alone. The church was part of the gospel. To be baptized was to enter into a community, and in that community they must continue till death; in it they must grow; through it they must witness. A solitary Christian was a contradiction in terms!

True, the *word* "church" only occurs twice in the gospels, but the *idea* is central to them. Jesus speaks of the *reign* of God; that reign implies a community in which God's rule is acknowl-~ edged. Jesus speaks of the *fatherhood* of God; and that implies a family over which the Father presides and for every member of which he cares. Jesus speaks of himself as the good *Shepherd;* and that implies a flock which he tends and for which he was prepared to give his life. All these are corporate concepts. A Christian is a member of a living, worshiping, praying, witnessing community.

When we turn to the Acts of the Apostles, the story of what happened when the physical presence of Jesus was withdrawn and the communion of the disciples was with an *unseen* Lord, we can watch the development of the church pretty clearly. Its members consisted mostly of very ordinary people—not many wise people by human standards, not many power- ful, not many highly born joined it at the start. But it spread like wildfire. Baptisms and conver- sions to Christ took place in center after center, until it reached the imperial capital, Rome, before long. Sometimes these little groups were founded by the preaching of outstanding figures like Peter and Paul; sometimes the seed was planted and watered by an ordinary Christian lay man or woman, perhaps a soldier, a merchant, or a housewife who, traveling for business or family reasons, "gossiped the gospel" in such a way that others heard and believed. The Acts of the Apostles—the title is a misnomer and the book should more accurately be called the Acts of the Holy Spirit—is an exciting bit of church history. Not that all is sunshine—far from it! These little churches were composed of people much like ourselves, prone to quarrel, liable to break up into parties or to succumb to jealousies. There is plenty of evidence of this, the more unsavory aspect of church life, in the stories told in the Acts. Nothing is glossed over. It's all very human and sometimes very humiliating. But in spite of it all, the church grows and spreads, and through it the light of the gospel shines.

Those of us who have to wrestle with the incubus of inherited buildings and structures, who have to work away at the problem of finance and manpower, may be inclined to sometimes envy those early communities who had no such problems to deal with. All they needed was a room lent to them for the purpose of their meeting, a bottle of wine and a loaf of bread to celebrate the Eucharist, and if possible a copy of the Scriptures from which to read. It was all very simple and uncomplicated from that point of view; though it must at once be added that the Christian in the Greco-Roman world had problems of persecution and misunderstanding of which we, at least in the West, know singularly little.

Well, there is the picture given to us in the *Acts*—progress, wonderful progress, but always in the face of opposition, sometimes from the world outside, sometimes from sin and weakness within.

When we come to the Epistles, we owe more to Paul when we seek to learn about the church. He seems to have spoken of it under three main metaphors.

First, he spoke of it as the *Bride* of Christ. This was a picture with which, in some ways, readers of the Old Testament would have been familiar. Israel was destined to be the bride of God. From that ideal she had all too often defected— "played the harlot" is how the prophets spoke of her sin. But God loved her and longed to woo her back. Paul sees the church as the Bride of Christ—the fair, spotless bride whom he loved and for whom he laid down His life—infinitely precious in his sight.

Secondly, Paul spoke of the church as the *Body* of Christ, each member being a limb, a constituent part with its own particular function to fulfill. Dependent on the head, Christ himself, each limb must function to the full if the body as a whole was to be healthy. Mutual interdependence and responsibility are clearly seen in this lively metaphor.

Thirdly, he speaks of the church as a *building,* Christ himself being the cornerstone which holds the structure together, the members being the stones of which it is built. The building grows as new members are added. It is strong or weak depending on whether its members fulfill the functions allotted to them in the maintenance and growth of the building. It grows, in order to become a spiritual dwelling for God through the Spirit, a holy temple in the Lord.

Bride, Body, Building—metaphors, pictures, just that, with all the limitations which metaphors necessarily have. But there is enough in them to show how one of the greatest thinkers of the early church conceived it—in its holiness, its growth, its glory.

Yes, its glory! And its shame. For we have already seen how often the members of the church spoiled things by their quarrels, their jealousies, their party spirit, their lack of unity. It's all there in the New Testament.

There is the paradox of the church—its glory and its shame. If you read its story down nineteen centuries and a half, both stand out a mile, the glory and the shame. The never-ceasing worship of Almighty God; the splendor of its missionary expansion; the compassionate service of its members; the educational, medical, and evangelistic work—here is its glory. And there is the shame of its sheer sinfulness, its smugness, its dividedness, in the face of which we can only pray, "Lord, have mercy."

The reformers of the sixteenth century used to make much of a phrase which described the Christian man as at once justified and a sinner, forgiven and yet always liable to sin, right with God and yet always prone to wrong. There is the razor edge of Christian experience. What is true of the individual is true also of the church. It is the Bride of Christ, his Body, his holy Building. But it is composed entirely of frail members of a sinful humanity. It's no use looking for the perfect church. At least it's no use *my* looking for it, for if I found it I could not be a member of it, for I am not perfect. True, thanks to the infinite mercy of God and the amazing grace of Christ, I can say that I am forgiven and so I can look into the face of God with confidence. But at the same time I am a sinner, only too liable to trip up, to disgrace my Lord, to weaken his church by my deliberate folly or my sheer neglect of duty. And what is true of me is true of all my fellow members of the Body of Christ.

None of us can afford to be censorious about the failures of the church, for if we are truly members of it we *are* part of the failure. There is a scandal to the church, and we must not seek to escape that scandal by standing on the sidelines in judgment. It is up to us to do our part, however small and apparently insignificant that part may be, in lessening the shame and adding to the glory.

Let's stop moaning about the church—universal or local. Let's stop pining for the good old days (*were* they so good, I wonder?). Let's stop wishing we hadn't got the problems which beset us—every age has presented the church with a set of new ones!

And let's begin to ask the really sensible questions:

Is my worship of the living God regular, lively, full of wonder?

Is my witness to Christ consistent and clear?

Am I a functioning limb in the Body of Christ?

Or has *this* bit of the Body had a stroke?

5. Love

There is a story in the Gospels of a lawyer who had been listening to some discussions which Jesus had been having with some religious leaders. He was impressed by the way in which Jesus handled the questions they posed. There was a depth to his teaching and a shrewdness to the way in which he avoided the traps they set him. The lawyer decided *he* would ask Jesus a question. Whether it was intended as a trap or whether it was propounded out of sincerity and a desire to reach the truth, the record does not say. I rather think it was the latter. "Which commandment is first of all?" That was his question. And our Lord's answer was: "The first is, 'Hear, O Israel: the Lord our God is the only Lord; love the Lord your God with all your heart, with all your soul, with all your mind, and with all your strength.' The second is this: 'Love your neighbour as yourself.' There is no other commandment greater than these" (NEB).

The answer was not original. It was a quotation straight out of the Old Testament, the book of Deuteronomy in fact.

It is interesting, isn't it, that Jesus did not answer by quoting the Ten Commandments. His not doing so does not mean that he did not approve of them. On the contrary, he claimed to have come to fulfill them. Those commandments are a kind of fence for society—of very great value in saving communities and individuals from falling over the edge of the precipice into disaster. There must be law in any healthy society, and the Ten Commandments are the rules by which society can live healthily and happily. If we neglect them or break them, we break ourselves and run into chaos.

But the Ten Commandments are largely negative. In his reply to the lawyer's question, Jesus quotes the two great positive commands—the love of God and love of neighbor.

However, there is more to it than this. There are three loves spoken of in the words Jesus quotes—love of God and love of neighbor and love of self—"Love your neighbour *as yourself.*"

Let us begin by reversing the order, and look at the three loves in inverse order to that in which Jesus spoke. This way we shall begin with what we are most familiar with—ourselves—and leave till last the most important—God.

On the face of it, it sounds surprising that, even if we are not specifically told to love ourselves, it is assumed that we do and we should. There is a passage in the Gospels in which Jesus, in referring to the cost of being one of his disciples, says that if a man does not hate his father and mother, yes, and himself as well, he cannot be a disciple. This is clearly hyperbolic language, the language of extreme exaggeration used to register a point of importance hard to understand. We need not, I think, take it as contradicting this reference to love our neighbor *as we love ourselves.*

What does it mean to love myself? Well, look at me. I am, from one point of view, a very insignificant bit of creation. Here for a brief space and then gone! As one of the psalmists put it, "a puff of wind," a passing shadow. My impact on world history is not very great! But in God's sight I am of immense importance. He thought enough of me to give his Son to die for me. I am made in the image of God. I am destined to be "shaped to the likeness of his Son." I am to be "like him," and eventually "to see him as he is." If this is so—and it is clearly the Bible's estimate of man's person and destiny—I can do no other than treat myself with the reverence—I use the word advisedly—the reverence due to a son of the Most High God. I must not despise myself, though I may have cause to despise some of the things which I do when I forget whose I am and whom I should be serving. I am one of God's athletes—in training to be the best for him, the best possible in mind and body and spirit. Even when I have sinned grievously, I must never say, "I can never forgive myself for that." God forgives me in his infinite mercy. Who am I to refuse to follow his example?

So, the love of self, so far from being an indulgence, is something which God expects from one made in his own image and redeemed with the blood of his Son.

Next we come to the command to "love your neighbour as yourself." Two questions present themselves: What is the meaning of *love?* and, Who is our neighbor?

It is a great pity that the word "love" has become so tarnished with usage. In our everyday parlance it can stand for everything from lust in its crudest form, through love in its highest human manifestation, to the love of God shown to us in Christ.

When Christians speak of love, they are thinking of something not primarily emotional. There is, of course, an emotional element to it—and it would be hard to conceive of a love which did not have that as a constituent part of it. But Christian love has much more to do with the will than with the emotions. Indeed, it has been defined as "the set of the will for the eternal welfare of another." That is a good description. That being so, it would be conceivable for me, at least in the early stages of a relationship, to love a person without actually liking him (I think the liking would pretty certainly follow, for love has a way of seeing the good in people which the loveless cannot glimpse).

"The *eternal* welfare," our definition said. That means that I treat the other as one who, like myself, is destined in the Mind of God to "enjoy him for ever," as the old catechism had it; destined to be redeemed, restored, forgiven;

destined to reach the goal as a son or daughter of the living God. Therefore his eternal welfare matters supremely—I can never use him as a thing for my pleasure or my profit. He is a person, just as precious to God as I am.

And *neighbor*—who is my neighbor? He may be my neighbor in the sense in which we now usually understand the word, the person next door, the person who occupies the apartment in the same block as mine, the person down the road. Jesus says I am to love that person. The truth is that very often we don't even get to *know* them! That is why a city can be the loneliest place on earth, and dwellers in great blocks of buildings the loneliest people on earth. We like to "keep ourselves to ourselves." Not much love of neighbor in that! There is even a married love which is selfish—two people so much in love with each other, so wrapped up in each other, that they have little room for anyone else. That is the love of one's closest neighbor which excludes other neighbors, a restricted, narrow love. And that is a warped kind of love.

But it is clear that when Jesus spoke of neighbor he was thinking in much wider terms than those I have just mentioned. In fact, one of his best known stories illustrates the point with uncomfortable clarity. "Who is my neighbor?" the lawyer asks, the neighbor mentioned in the two great commandments. Jesus answers not directly but by telling a story which would get his questioner thinking furiously. He tells of a man, presumably a Jew, going down to Jericho and falling into the hands of robbers, bandits, guerrillas, who strip him and leave him on the road half dead. A priest going down the road takes one look at the pathetic figure. Was he dead? Alive? He couldn't tell, and anyway he must be on his way to church—so he passes by on the other side. So does another very religious type, a Levite. Then along comes another man, of all things a Samaritan! He takes a look, drops his work, attends to the bleeding man, puts him on his donkey, takes him to the nearby hotel, pays for his keep there, and promises to look in again on his way back. Which of these three was neighbor? The question answers itself.

But there is a sting to the story. Jews and Samaritans were sworn enemies; they hated each other like poison. But *love* overlooks, takes no notice of differences of nationality. *Need* is the criterion. If Jesus had been telling the tale in Israel today, I suppose the Samaritan would have been an Arab. If he had been in Britain, the Samaritan would have been a Pakistani. If he had been in Cape Town, the Samaritan would have been a black. In short, in God's vocabulary a neighbor is anyone, yes anyone, in need of my compassion.

Now we come to the first and greatest command—to love *God*. What does *this* mean? Here again, as in the case of love of neighbor, *will* prevails over emotion. When I am at my coldest, when I don't *feel* any warmth of love for

God, I can still love him with mind and will. The Bible, and perhaps especially John in his first letter, is very down-to-earth about this. He insists on the sheer impossibility of loving God, whom we have not seen, if we don't love our neighbor, whom we have seen—I suppose he would add, if he had been writing today, seen in person or on a television screen. Is this a glimpse of the obvious? The point certainly needs making!

If you love somebody, you want to spend time in his company. If you are not sure about somebody or have your suspicions about him, the best thing to do is to spend some time in his company and get to know him; that way, you very often find that your suspicions have little foundation to them—he's nicer than you thought he was! Some of us have grave suspicions about God—his justice, his love, his care. Why has he done this, or behaved toward us like that? Some of us have grown up with childish ideas of him which we have never outgrown; sometimes those ideas are monstrously unfair to him and untrue about him. It's high time that we spent some time in his company, in a conscious endeavor to get to know him. Of course we shall need help—help perhaps in using silence with a simple prayer like this: "O God, if you are there, make yourself known to me"; or, "Lord, have mercy on me, a sinner"; or the use of the name of *Jesus,* just by itself— there's power in that name.

We may need the help of others—a priest or a godly lay man or woman, a friend who is obviously a Christian disciple. We may find that a prayerful use of a bit of one of the Gospels or of the Epistles will help, or the reading of a book written by one who knows and loves God better than we do. By these or other means a tiny flame of love for God often begins to burn; and when that happens, there is no knowing what it will lead to!

We have inverted our Lord's order in his reply to the lawyer because we wanted to begin with the known and work toward the unknown. We have thought of love of self, of neighbor, and of God. His order was, of course, the right one. The most important of the three is love of *God.* But here we are up against a snag. The truth is that, in our natural state, we are lacking in love. A command like this—love of God and love of neighbor—is totally impossible of achievement unless a miracle takes place, unless God in his mercy will give me an in-filling of his own love. "Lord, my dykes are dry. Come, Holy Spirit, fill me with your own great love." That is a prayer which God is always glad to answer, a request he is always glad to grant. "The love of God is shed abroad in our hearts by the Holy Spirit given to us."

"Come, Holy Ghost, our souls inspire."

6. Faith

It would not be right—it would be scarcely possible—to consider the great words of life without including among their number the word *faith.* It is a word Christians are always talking about—sometimes, we must admit, without being quite sure what they mean by it.

It is, of course, a word which is by no means exclusively religious. We've all heard people say, "I've got great faith in my doctor"; or "I've faith in what my stockbroker advises me"; and we know what they mean. These people are experts in their field. They are persons of integrity. They can be trusted. We put our body—in the case of the doctor—in their hands with confidence; our money, in the case of the stockbroker. This use of the word will give us a clue to the meaning of the word in a religious context, and we'll come back to it shortly.

It's funny, isn't it, how, when we think of the term in a religious context, we often get it wrong? We laugh at the schoolboy's definition of faith as "believing what you know to be untrue," but there is just enough in his definition to make us stop and think for a minute. For all too many people do seem to believe—though they probably wouldn't admit it—that being a Christian, a person of faith, means doing despite to your intelligence, saying good-bye to your intellect, taking a deep breath, and swallowing the lot—"the lot" being a hodgepodge of ill-digested and ill-considered credal assortments! God is the God of truth, and he never—no, never—asks us to do despite to the intelligence he gave us. Our intelligence will not take us all the way in our relationship with him. More than that is called for. But so far from his expecting us to say good-bye to our intellect when we become Christian disciples, he expects us to use all we have got in the way of thinking and reasoning powers.

Let's take a very brief look at the way in which the word "faith" is used in the New Testament. It is used in three ways.

First, it is used in the sense of faithfulness or reliability. It is an ethical idea. Thus, when Paul is describing the kind of character which the Holy Spirit produces in the person who belongs to God, he says that one of his marks, of his characteristics, is faithfulness. His word is as good as his bond. You can bet your shirt on him. He won't let you down.

Secondly, it is used (but very rarely) in the sense of The Faith, the body of Christian belief, almost the Christian religion.

Thirdly—and this is by far and away the most frequent use—it means trust in a person, supremely trust in God or in the Person of Christ through whom we come to God.

Now it is in this last sense that we come closest to the use of the word I spoke about a moment ago: "I've complete trust in my doctor, or in my stockbroker." This is a relationship between two people. Let's look at the doctor-patient relationship for a moment. Here is a man who is obviously sick. He knows it and admits it, but he can't do much about it because he's not an expert. So he goes to one. Perhaps a friend who has been operated on and cured by this doctor recommends him. He determines to try him. Soon he finds he was not ill-advised. The doctor is clearly an expert—you can tell by the way he asks questions, diagnoses, prescribes, and, maybe, operates. The proof of his expertise is seen when health comes stealing—or flooding—back again. "I can trust that man," the patient says.

Now we pass from our medical illustration to the New Testament. Here is a young man in tremendous form, as he thinks, *spiritually*. He is outwardly very religious—he was brought up that way. He has fulfilled all the demands of his religion—at least the outward demands. In fact, young as he is, he is already becoming a very considerable leader; and in addition, he has been to a couple of universities and sat at the feet of some of the most eminent teachers. "What a man!" say all his friends, and clap him on the back.

He himself, however, suspects that all is not as well as others think. There were things his friends didn't know about but which he *did*—his religious pride in his own achievements; but how did that look in the eyes of God? The hatred of the Christians which gnawed at his vitals! And why was it that every night, as he lay and tossed on his bed, he saw once again the face of Stephen, angel-like, and heard him say: "Lord, lay not this sin to their charge"; it was just like what he had heard people affirm that Jesus had said when people were killing *him.* Conscience was getting busy. The Holy Spirit was at work. And Saul knew that all was not well. What would all his religious achievements look like in the eyes of a holy God? It was no use trusting to *them!* And then he saw it in a flash—there was only One totally reliable in whom he could trust, the ultimate Expert who could handle man's dis-ease and put him right and bring him peace with himself, with others, and with his God. It was the Jesus, the Christ, the Lord, the Lord Jesus Christ, whom he hitherto had been persecuting, whom now he was trusting.

A few years later, he found himself writing to some of his friends: "To me, life *is* Christ." "The life which I now live in the flesh—my present bodily life—is lived by faith in the Son of God, who loved me and gave himself up for me." That is faith— a very personal relationship between a person and God in Christ; the transference of trust from fallible, sinful self to the totally reliable God. When that happens, a miracle happens. The floodgates of God's love and joy and peace are opened, and a man finds himself no longer battling on alone but with the powers of Christ's Spirit at work in him and the fellowship of the household of faith available to him.

"The household of faith"—I like that description of the church of God. I have so far spoken of faith in a very personal way—the relationship of trust between a sick person and his doctor, or between a sinner and his Savior. And that is right. But if that relationship is to develop and deepen, it will be developed and deepened within the community of which Christ is Lord and of which the other "faith-men," the other believers, are members. "The grace of our Lord Jesus Christ, and the love of God" are experienced within "the fellowship of the Holy Spirit." There the Word of God is proclaimed and expounded. There the sacraments are administered—the sacrament of incorporation, of cleansing, of dying in Christ and rising again, the sacrament of *baptism;* and the sacrament of the *eucharist,* where Christ's men and women feed on him in their hearts by faith with thanksgiving. There we learn from one another, in prayer and study and conversation and witness and service, we learn how little we know, how much there is to learn. There we glimpse something of the many-colored wisdom of God and begin to know the love of Christ which passes knowledge. There we begin to explore what it means to be "in Christ"—a kind of co-inherence such as two lovers experience as they get to know one another at deeper and deeper levels. In that fellowship of the household of faith we appreciate something of the meaning of Paul's amazing statement that "it is God himself who called us to share in the life of his Son Jesus Christ our Lord; and God keeps faith."

That's what it is all about—the totally reliable God, the immensity of whose faithfulness is there to meet my feeble trust.

He who calls you is to be trusted; he will do it.

7. Grace

Next to the Lord's Prayer, the "Our Father," the prayer best known to the Christian is the one we call "The Grace." It runs: "The grace of our Lord Jesus Christ, and the love of God, and the fellowship of the Holy Spirit, be with you all." It is a very ancient Christian prayer. It was composed and came into use only two or three decades after the death of Jesus on the Cross. The Christians who, at the start, were mostly Jews and, of course, very strong monotheists (only one God for them!), found themselves, when they knelt to pray, seeing the face of Jesus. They found themselves praying to *him*. In fact, the first martyr of the Christian church, Stephen, when he was being stoned to death, prayed not as Jesus had done by addressing God as Father but by addressing Jesus—"Lord Jesus, receive my spirit!" That is a very remarkable fact.

If you had asked an early Christian to rationalize this, to explain what had happened, I think he might have said something like this: "No man has seen God at any time. There is one of our difficulties. What is he like? Is he capricious? Or can he be trusted? Is he to be appeased? Or is he to be loved? No man has seen God. But we have been in touch with One called Jesus. He came from Nazareth. He was a workman. He went about doing good, teaching, preaching, healing. He died on the Cross a most horrible death at the hands of the authorities. Men did their worst to him—and he took it all. Yet somehow *God* was in on that. There on the Cross God was in Christ reconciling the world to himself. He vindicated all that Jesus was and did by raising him from the dead. It is perfectly true that his physical presence is withdrawn. We see him no more. But though we don't see him, we love him. We can never forget him. But he is much more to us than a memory—he is with us; indeed, in a very real sense, *in* us. No wonder when we pray we see him, Jesus of Nazareth, crucified, risen, alive. His graciousness has shown us what God is like. We can now believe in the love of God in a way we couldn't do before we saw Jesus with our own eyes, heard him, looked upon him, felt him. It's natural, isn't it, that if in our praying we are thinking about the *love* of God, we should preface it with a reference to the *grace* of our Lord Jesus Christ. He was—and he is—our way in to an understanding of God. Indeed, he is our way in to the Presence of God."

Yes, I think an early Christian might have said something like this if you had asked him how he came to pray to Jesus and why he put the grace of the Lord Jesus before the love of God in that well-known prayer that I've been talking about.

How are we to define "grace"? Well, how define the sunrise? But let's have a try. In its un-theological sense it simply means graceful-ness. We might say of a beautiful woman that she carries herself with great grace. Or, of a speaker whose words make a great appeal to his hearers, we could use the same word. In fact, Luke, in describing the effect of Jesus' first sermon preached in his home town of Nazareth, says that "all eyes in the synagogue were fixed on him. . . . There was a general stir of admira-tion; they were surprised that words of such grace should fall from his lips" (NEB). We can understand that. Religion to him was no harsh, legalistic thing. It was lovely; it was gracious. Coming from him, it made a strong appeal to them.

That is the simplest, face-value sense of the word. Then it began to take on fuller and deeper meanings as people pondered more deeply the meaning not only of the teaching of Jesus but of his own Person and work. "You know the grace of our Lord Jesus Christ," Paul said in one of his letters. Yes, they knew that—the graciousness of his every word and deed. But here Paul defines that grace more closely—"that, though he was rich, yet for your sakes he became poor, that ye through his poverty might be rich." In other words, grace is something which can only be understood if it is seen in action. Grace is giving, self-giving, self-giving to the uttermost.

In the case of God, grace often takes the form

of forgiveness. There is an interesting story which Jesus once told in one of his parables. He told of a man to whom two other men were in debt. One owed a colossal sum; the other a comparatively paltry one. But they were both in the same boat—they were both flat broke, both totally bankrupt. What was the man to do? He might, according to the custom of the day, clap them both into jail. Or he might, I suppose, make them set about the process of trying to pay back what they owed—quite likely a sheer impossibility. He took neither course. "He *graced* them both," says the parable. "He forgave them both." They could do nothing but accept the man's graciousness with infinite gratitude, and go out to start a new life under, I imagine, a totally new relationship with the man who had "graced" them.

Forgiveness is a costly thing. You know that if you have ever forgiven anyone who has deeply hurt you or wronged you. A costly forgiveness lies at the heart of the Christian gospel. It is the love of God in action, going out to man in his need of forgiveness. Love doesn't constantly reckon up the long list of our sins and refuse to do anything about us till we improve. If that were the case, we should indeed be in a bad way. Here is one of the great differences between the Old Testament and the New. In the Old Testament we are told over and over that "the Lord loves the *righteous*." The New Testament gives us the joyous assurance that while we were yet *sinners,* Christ died for us—such was the measure of his love! The picture of the Good Shepherd who is not content with the ninety-nine safely in the fold, who does not wait for the hundredth sheep to find its own way back, but rather leaves the ninety-nine in their security and breasts the dangers of wind and precipice and searches for the sheep until he finds it—this is the good news of the gospel. What should I have had to say to the young alcoholic who came to see me recently, having made a mess of his life, and who said to me, "Will God really forgive me all the awful things I have done?"—what should I have said if I had not believed the utter truth of the forgiveness of sins, at the cost of Christ's death, and the basic truth of the grace of God, God's love in action going out to people like that alcoholic and to me? He and I—both of us—need more than a teacher, more than an example, more than a code of ethics. We need a Savior who in infinite mercy goes out after us, even when we have run away from him. All he asks is that we turn around and face him and throw ourselves into the arms of his mercy.

Sometimes these very deep and wonderful things can best be expressed in poetry. I do not pretend that the poems you are now going to read are poetry at its most sublime, but I find them moving in the way that they get to the heart of this matter of grace, about which we are thinking.

Here is one:

There were ninety and nine that safely lay
   In the shelter of the fold,
But one was out on the hills away,
   Far off from the gates of gold;
Away on the mountains wild and bare,
Away from the tender Shepherd's care.

"Lord, thou hast here thy ninety and nine;
   Are they not enough for thee?"
But the Shepherd made answer: "This of mine
   Has wandered away from me;
And although the road be rough and steep,
I go to the desert to find my sheep."

But none of the ransomed ever knew
   How deep were the waters crossed;
Nor how dark the night that the Lord
     passed through
   Ere he found his sheep that was lost.
Out in the desert he heard its cry—
Sick and helpless and ready to die.

"Lord, whence are those blood-drops all the way,
   That mark out the mountain's track?"
"They were shed for one that had gone astray
   Ere the Shepherd could bring him back."
"Lord, whence are thy hands so rent and torn?"
"They are pierced tonight by many a thorn."

And all through the mountains, thunder-riven,
   And up from the rocky steep,
There rose a cry to the gates of heaven:
   "Rejoice! I have found my sheep!"

And the angels echoed around the throne:
"Rejoice! for the Lord brings back his own."
(Elizabeth C. Clephane)

And here is part of another:

My song is love unknown,
My Saviour's love to me,
Love to the loveless shown,
That they might lovely be.
O who am I,
That for my sake
My Lord should take
Frail flesh, and die?

He came from his blest throne,
Salvation to bestow;
But men made strange, and none
The longed-for Christ would know.
But O, my Friend,
My Friend indeed,
Who at my need
His life did spend!
(Samuel Crossman)

8. Peace

I can still remember—just remember—the day when the First World War broke out. I was a little under five years of age, and my father announced that he was to be a Special Constable. That is to say that, in the absence of many men at the front, he would do his little bit at home in a kind of part-time help to the police force. And I can remember the ending of the First World War—I must have been nine—and the utter relief that came, after the holocaust, with peace. Twenty years passed, and another horror was launched on the world. Six years more, and another world sigh of relief. Peace had come!

To those of us who have lived through experiences such as these, or who have watched from a distance the battles in Vietnam or the hostilities in the Near East or in Ireland, the word "peace," in the sense of a cessation of hostilities, is a magic word of almost unutterable beauty. "Blessed are the peacemakers"; we echo the words of Jesus as we watch a foreign secretary shuttle to and fro on his peace errands, or as we admire the initiative of a President Sadat in making a breakthrough.

In the Christian religion and in the Bible, the idea of peace occupies a prominent place. The Old Testament has its full share of "battles long ago," often pretty bloody ones, and of peace after war. Those stories may or may not interest you; it depends largely on whether you are interested in ancient history. But at a deeper level, the Bible has much to say about peace which is of immense relevance to every one of us.

First of all, it speaks about a man's *peace with God.* The Bible takes with full seriousness the fact of man's opposition to God—his rebellion against God. Jesus seems to have been very conscious of this side of human nature. He told a parable of a landowner who let out his vineyard to vine-growers whose responsibility it was to look after it during his absence and to see that the land produced its proper crops. Sending his servants to receive the fruits, he found that they were treated with hostility by the tenants and sent away maltreated and empty-handed. He did this more than once—and the same results ensued. Last of all he sent his son, saying: "They will reverence my son." But the tenants conspired together and killed the son. There was rebellion in the hearts of men. They were at war with the boss.

When we speak of man's hostility to God, we do not deny for one moment the great yearning love of God for men. That goes on—and on. "Christ died for us while we were yet sinners, and that is God's own proof of his love towards us." But—and we are reminded of this too seldom—God is a God of love *and of holiness.* Holiness is the other side of the coin of the love of God. And where God's holiness and man's sin meet, there is bound to be flame, judgment, opposition. It cannot be otherwise. The meeting place of holiness and sin must always be an awful place. That is why heaven—for a sinner who has not had his sin problem dealt with— must be hell. He could not stand the holiness of the love of God.

But Christ came to preach peace to us who by our nature are at cross-purposes with God. Indeed, he himself *is* our peace. So there is a ring of intense joy and confidence when Paul writes to his friends: "Now that we have been justified through faith, let us continue at peace with God through our Lord Jesus Christ, through whom we have been allowed to enter the sphere of God's grace, where we now stand" (NEB). This entirely new relationship of a man with God comes about not through that man's efforts or achievements, but by God's outgoing love accepted by an unworthy recipient. It is when we reach the point of realizing our utter need that the grace of God can operate and we can enter a new relationship of peace with God.

Then, *secondly,* the Bible has much to say about peace in our interpersonal relationships, peace one with another. Perhaps a diagram, easily pictured without the aid of a blackboard, will help us. Here is a triangle. At the apex is God, at one of the base points is my neighbor, at the other myself. That is all. If I am in wrong relationship with my neighbor, an effect takes place automatically in my relationship with God. To sin against my neighbor—be that neighbor my wife, my employer, my employee, or whoever—is to sin against God. To be in a wrong relationship with someone is to spoil my relationship with God, so closely interrelated are the three points of the triangle one to another.

That is why, when someone wants to get right with God, he often has first at least to do his part in righting a wrong relationship with a relation or a friend. This may entail the writing of a letter, the making of an apology, or the return of some money or property wrongly obtained. Once peace is made with one's neighbor, peace with God frequently follows. Many a spiritual life has died for a man or a woman because of some sin unconfessed. Put that right, and prayer and communion with God come alive.

It is in the purpose of God that constantly and all over the world, communities should grow up of men and women living in a relationship of peace and love with one another and with him—redeemed and redeeming fellowships, the members of which are so at peace that they can reach out in loving activity to others, win them, and draw them into larger communities where the transforming power of God is at work.

Peace with God. Peace in our interpersonal relationships in our community living. And *thirdly, peace with my own self.* If you read the Gospels, you must be impressed with the fact that so often, when Jesus came into close contact with an individual, he brought peace to that individual. I need only give a couple of examples.

Here was a man distraught, deranged, at war with himself. When Jesus asked him his name, he replied, "Legion, for we are many." No inner harmony; only a cacophony of discordant voices and desires. No unity of purpose leading to a life of fulfillment, but inner warfare leading to madness. Jesus deals with him as tenderly as a mother deals with her child, as firmly as a surgeon with his patient. The man called Legion ceases to be a mob and becomes once again a man. Peace reigns within—the peace of forgiveness, of reinstatement with God, of wholeness, of holiness.

And there is the other story of a woman, this time a woman whom Jesus met by the well of Sychar, probably more sinned against than sinning, but a poor wreck of a human being. So ashamed she was, that she would not come to draw water in the morning but came, rather, in the noonday heat, to avoid the jeers and insults of the others who came with their water-pots. But Jesus, meeting her there alone, forgetting his own weariness and the heat of the day, sensed that the woman had no peace, and laid himself out to bring it to her. She went away whole, holy, the kind of woman God made her to be. Peace reigned within.

Let us make no mistake. Such peace is not a selfish thing. It is the most unselfish thing in the world. You cannot minister to others in their need if you yourself are in turmoil. You cannot bring rest to others if you yourself are storm-tossed. You will be effective in rescuing others in distress when your own feet are firm on the Rock which is Christ.

One of Paul's finest prayers runs like this: "The peace of God, which passes all under-standing, keep your hearts and minds in the knowledge and love of God and of His Son Jesus Christ our Lord." "Keep"—the word means *garrison.* I need not comment on *that!*

> Peace does not mean the end of all our striving;
> Joy does not mean the drying of our tears;
> Peace is the power that comes to souls arriving
> Up to the light where God Himself appears.
> (G. A. Studdert-Kennedy)

9. Life

A court jester was once called to the bedside of the king to beguile his sadness. The jester's mirth, however, failed for once. His best quips drew no corresponding smile from the king's pallid face. "Master," said the jester, "why so sad?" "Because," replied the king, "I have to leave my home and people and go on a journey." "Is it a long journey?" asked the jester. "It is indeed; the longest journey any man could take." "When are you going?" inquired the clown. "I don't know for certain, but I think it will be quite soon, now." "And what of your majesty's preparations?" continued the jester. "I see no clothing laid out, no boxes in the hall, no horses in the courtyard." "Alas!" was the reply. "You speak the truth. I have had so much else to occupy me that I have made no preparations for departure." "Then take my cap and bells," said the bold jester. "I thought I was the court fool, but I see there lies here a greater fool than I, since he is going on the longest journey man ever took, and yet calls he me here to beguile his precious moments with jest and tale, instead of preparing for his travels."

It is a good story, a telling tale—a pointed one, if you believe, as I do, that there is a journey of supreme importance when this little life is through.

Of course, some people do not believe this. Many say they don't. Bertrand Russell used to say, "When I die, I rot" (though it is interesting that, on his deathbed, he asked a friend of mine, a Christian layman, to pray with him).

Christians, of course, say they do believe in life after death. They affirm that belief every time they say the Creed—"I believe in . . . the life everlasting." It is the last of the affirmations of the Creed, and I must confess that sometimes—not always!—the way it is said reminds one more of the running down of an LP record than the declaration of a glorious truth! When it *is* said halfheartedly, it may reflect an uncertainty of belief which I have found in many people who would be insulted if there was any suggestion of their not being Christians!

How can we best set about looking at this matter? That it is one of importance the jester in the story clearly saw. That it is a difficult one no one will deny. No ordinary human being has been down into the valley of death and come back to tell us, with clarity, what it is like "over there." Where shall we begin?

Let us begin with the Old Testament. There we shall find very little indeed to help us. We shall find a great deal about "going down into silence" where there is no praising of God, nothing to look forward to. In the very latest books of the Old Testament and in the books which we call the Apocrypha—they are not included in *most* of our Bibles with the other books—a picture of life after death begins to emerge; but, as I say, that is getting pretty close to the New Testament period.

What we do find in the Old Testament is an almost desperate stress on the desire of continuity of the family line. Father will die, and that, so far as he can tell, will be the end. So he must ensure that his life is continued in his children and grandchildren. This desire for continuity through the family accounts for much of the horror which is attached to sterility and infertility. For a woman to be barren (and the people of those days knew little about male infertility) was the greatest curse she could bear. It is interesting that in a recent issue of the *Journal of Medical Ethics,* the writer of an "agony column" in one of our popular papers pointed out how many people today are "quite literally frantic with fear at any threat to their ability to have babies." She went on: "I think it is perhaps because the vast majority of people who write to me make it clear that children are the only hope they have of continuance. People who are blessed with a deep religious faith that offers them the comfort of knowing they have an everlasting soul may not need the concrete evidence of immortality that children provide, but for the childless non-believer death indeed comes as the end."

To return to the Bible. The period between the Old Testament and the New was one of intense distress for the Jewish people. They were harassed. They were persecuted. They were killed in cold blood and in great numbers. And many of those who were martyred were done to death just because they refused to give up the practice of their religion and to abandon their faith in the God of Abraham, Isaac, and Jacob. This presented the most acute theological, religious, and ethical problem. Where was the God of the prophets—the God of justice and of love? Why didn't he do something about the appalling events of which his people were helpless spectators? As they wrestled with this problem—the justice and righteousness of God and the sin and cruelty of man—there began to emerge, out of the midst of their agony, a doctrine of an afterlife, of a heaven and a hell. True, it was sometimes a pretty crude picture which was painted. Sometimes there was an ugly color of vengeance about it. But at least it was an attempt to face a problem and find an answer. In the New Testament we have a purified and developed doctrine, but its origins are found in an attempt at what the theologians call a theodicy, the justifying of the ways of God with man. After all, what do *you* think about the problem—*are* we all going the same way? Once again, do Hitler and Mother Theresa have the same destination? If they do, what do you think your God is like?

We have spoken of man's longing for *continuance* and his longing for *justice.* Now we must look a little closer at what a Christian means when he speaks of everlasting life. There is, of course, a strong note of continuity of existence in the word "everlasting." Not, indeed, continuity of the body which has served him for a longer or a shorter period of years with greater or lesser efficiency. That will dissolve. But that is not he; it is only part of him, the temporal part. "Flesh and blood will not enter the kingdom of God." When a Christian speaks of everlasting life, he means much more than continuity of living. He is thinking of *quality* of life, the quality of a relationship with God which, having begun and been nurtured in this life, continues and flourishes in the next.

A relationship, I said. At the heart of the Christian faith is the conviction that it is possible—yes, more than this, that it is the will of God—for men and women to enter into a relationship of love and trust with God through Jesus Christ, and, as a member of his church, to grow in grace and knowledge. "To as many as received him," John wrote, "to them gave he power to become the sons of God, even to them that believe on his name." To live in that relationship with God, to nourish and develop it by prayer and sacrament and service, is to enter into Life. That living relationship cannot be terminated just because the *body* of the believer is tired and has to be sloughed off. In a way which it is not possible fully to imagine, it will continue in the next stage. "There are many dwelling-places in my Father's house" (NEB) —could we say "stages"?

It is at this point that language and imagination let us down. What exactly will heaven be like? I don't know. The Bible tries to depict it in language that to its original readers would be meaningful. There will be no sea—of course not, for the Jews were land-lovers and hated the sea. There will be no sunshine that will burn and weary—they lived in a climate that could be cruelly hot. The pavements will be of gold—they were mostly very poor. It will be like one great city—they needed the security of community life. And so on and so on. The language is meaningful, but only up to a point.

What I believe can be universally understood in its outline—it might well take eternity fully to comprehend it—is the kind of thing that Paul says when he speaks of the Christian's destiny as being shaped to the likeness of God's Son. For the Christian man or woman, that process is now proceeding. Our characters are being molded in a Christ-like way. But there are many snags in the way, and sometimes the progress seems disappointingly slow. Heaven, according to this way of thinking, will be the state in which this process goes on, without let or hindrance. The relationship will deepen, and none shall stop it.

Or we could put it in the language of John in his first Letter: "How great is the love that the Father has shown to us! We were called God's children, and such we are. . . . Here and now . . . we are God's children; what we shall be has not yet been disclosed"—I like that honest bit of "agnosticism"!—"but we know that when it is disclosed we shall be like him, because we shall see him as he is" (NEB). *"We shall be like him"*—that is heaven. And to be unlike him is hell. Imagine a man who has no thought for God, no love of God, who has never worshiped, served, and loved him—imagine such a man being ushered into the burning purity of his presence. It would indeed be hell!

We shall see him, we shall be like him, we shall be with him—that is what I mean by the continuation and deepening of a relationship. The dying thief, strung up on his wretched cross, began, at the last moment of his miserable life, a relationship with the Man on the Cross next to him. And at once came the assurance—from one dying Man to another—from the reigning Son of God to the dying but penitent thief—"Today thou shalt be with me." If that be true, death is not the end. It is a new beginning of unimaginable possibilities. It is a door.

One closing word. Continuation of relationship with Christ but on a higher plane surely implies a similar continuation of relationship

with others who are in Christ. The family of God
is not broken by death.

> He wants not friends that hath thy love,
> And may converse and walk with thee,
> And with thy saints here and above,
> With whom for ever I must be.
>
> As for my friends, they are not lost;
> The several vessels of thy fleet,
> Though parted now, by tempests tost,
> Shall safely in the haven meet.
>
> Still we are centred all in thee,
> Members, though distant, of one head;
> In the same family we be,
> By the same faith and spirit led.
>
> Before thy throne we daily meet
> As joint-petitioners to thee;
> In spirit we each other greet,
> And shall again each other see.
>
> (Richard Baxter)

10. Suffering

Anyone who attempts to deal with the subject of suffering in brief compass lays himself open to the charge of rashness, if not of sheer folly. On the other hand, anyone who, down the years, has lectured or spoken about suffering knows how big a response such a venture calls forth. To many, particularly to those who are sensitively made, the subject of suffering raises questions which refuse to be silenced, and often they are questions which are an obstacle to faith. If from the Cross there went up the anguished cry "My God, my God, why . . . ?" it is scarcely to be wondered at if that cry is wrung from those like ourselves from time to time, indeed very often.

The sheer size, the immensity of the problem, baffles us. Earthquakes, disasters, torturings, unjust imprisonments, disease—they scream at us from our television sets and from the headlines of our newspapers. Where is *God* in all this?

Let me say from the outset, anyone with an easy answer is not worth listening to. Nor is the man who treats this subject just as a philosophical conundrum. He is only worth listening to who has himself suffered, if not physically then at least nervously and spiritually, and who has sought to enter into the sufferings of others and to minister to them.

In this brief chapter, I must restrict myself to the more personal aspect of our problem—the subject of personal suffering of mind and/or of body. And I must restrict myself, very largely, to asking if the New Testament, and particularly the Gospels, have any light to shed, and if so, what is the nature of that light?

Let us watch Jesus at work with suffering humanity, so far as that picture is given us in the Gospels. I note four points:

1. Jesus struck a blow at the current Jewish doctrine which viewed suffering as invariably the consequence of sin, either on the part of the sufferer or of his forbears. The clearest case of this is the story of the man born blind recorded in the ninth chapter of John. Life makes it pretty obvious that frequently the proposition that suffering is the result of sin is true. But not invariably. If it be objected that the story gives us no positive philosophy of evil and of suffering, it may be replied that nowhere in the recorded sayings of Jesus is such a philosophy to be found; but, negative though the blow be which the story strikes, it removes at one stroke much of the bitterness which the current theory caused and, it may be added, still causes, in the minds of multitudes.

2. Jesus when faced by physical and mental

sickness almost invariably showed himself a fighter. So far as we can judge from the Gospels, it would appear that for Jesus to be *con*fronted by disease was to be *af*fronted. The Oxford English Dictionary defines "to affront" as to "insult to the face . . . to put to the blush . . . to cause to feel ashamed." Our Lord meets a poor woman with a twisted body (Luke 13:11). What does he do? Sigh, and pass by? Oh, no. Such a state of things he feels to be an affront to the plan of God, and an insult to his face. "This woman . . . Satan hath bound." He heals her, and she finds her body not a hindrance to the service of God but an expression of his glory.

Again, Mark (1:40) gives us the story of the leper who came to Jesus. He records the compassion with which Jesus viewed the pitiable figure. But in a well-known variant reading no compassion is recorded but rather anger. Judging by the canon of criticism which lays it down that the more difficult reading is the more likely, it is more probable that Jesus showed anger than compassion according to this story. We may well ask at what or at whom was Jesus thus incensed? Not at the by-standers (as in the story of the healing of the man with the withered hand—Mark 3:5), for no mention is made of them. Perhaps the anger of Jesus expressed the divine anger against sin, of which leprosy, a living death, spoke. But is it not more likely that the record of this anger is the Evangelist's attempt to express the reaction, the shame, which Jesus felt at the utter wrongness of the havoc wrought by sickness on the miracle which is a man's body? These instances—and there are others worthy of careful study—show us One who, so far from showing any resignation to suffering and death, seems to have opposed them with all the power at his command. He was a fighter against those elements in life which detracted from man's fullness of life, from his full health, from his "salvation." I may add in passing that to many of us this second point which I am making would be an indication of the way in which doctors and clergy should work together in the closest possible cooperation inasmuch as both are involved in an attack on all that cramps man's growth and development and peace.

3. Jesus refused in his healing work to concentrate solely upon the ills of the body. A paralytic is brought on his mattress bed (Mark 2:1). He looks expectantly to Jesus for physical healing. What must have been his surprise when Jesus said to him, not "your paralysis is cured" but "your sins are forgiven"! The great Physician diagnosed the trouble which underlay the outward manifestation, which was the physical paralysis. He saw that if there was to be a complete and permanent cure, the *whole* man must be dealt with. First, his relationship to God and to his fellows must be put right, then his physical healing would follow and there would go to his house a man every whit whole.

Again, the story of a demon-possessed man, told as it is no doubt only in outline (Mark 5:1-20), reminds us almost of a modern psychiatrist's approach to his patient. Jesus is apparently at considerable pains to get alongside the deranged man. He sympathetically questions him—"What is your name?" and elicits the significant answer of what sounds like a schizophrenic: "My name is Legion, for we are many." After the cure, Doctor and patient are together, presumably in close conclave. ("They came to Jesus and saw him that was possessed, sitting.") Mere expulsion of the demons was not enough. The man must feel that he is understood. He must be made whole in the totality of his personality.

The importance of this point can hardly be exaggerated. Any healing movement which simply goes out to cure physical sickness without reference to the well-being of the whole personality will have results compared with which the efforts of a bull in a china shop will be pacific. For if, as we have seen, it is true that suffering is not *invariably* the consequence of sin, it is also equally true that time and time again suffering is the manifestation in the physical part of him of a person's maladjustment to God, to his environment, or to himself. To attempt to cure the symptom without dealing with the root of the problem is like putting on a new tile to the roof when the foundations of the building are totally inadequate. When Jesus healed a man's or a woman's body or mind, that healing was one of the ways, one of the most expressive and eloquent ways, in which the Love of God in him went out to folk in need. But the God who made man as a psychosomatic unity loves that man in his entirety, and, if we may say so reverently, is all out for his total restoration. It was a wise French clinician who said: "There are no sicknesses, only sick people."

4. Jesus' greatest contribution in the realm of suffering was not what he did in healing, nor what he taught by word, but what he was in his person. The picture which the early documents give of Jesus is not of some superb Apollo, though it may be noted that we have no record of any sickness of Jesus but have, rather, the impression of one perfectly integrated and supremely at peace with God and with himself. Rather do the documents stress the fact that he whose name was Immanuel entered into our griefs with a terrible intimacy. Matthew, after recording Christ's healing of a leper, of the centurion's servant, of Peter's mother-in-law, and of the demon-possessed, concludes the section by recalling the words of Isaiah and noting their fulfillment in our Lord: "Himself took our infirmities, and bare our sicknesses" (8:17). He was indeed, as he himself taught, the suffering Servant foreshadowed in the great prophecies of Isaiah. It is the function of the *servants* in society to carry the burdens and to do the dirty work of mankind. Here, it seems to me,

we have a strong suggestion that anyone who is to get to grips with man's sickness needs more than technical skill, more even than a bedside manner; needs, indeed, a measure of that sympathy which means literally *suffering with* the person concerned.

I have just said, referring to our Lord Jesus Christ, "he entered into our griefs with a terrible intimacy." We cannot begin fully to enter into the darkness which surrounded the Cross on which Jesus died. But this we do know—that there he stood in with us, suffering as none of us ever will, bearing the load of our sin and shame and sorrow. "Having loved his own which were in the world, he loved them unto the end" (John 13:1). The Christian, who believes that God was in Christ reconciling the world to himself, has a God who did not, and does not, stand aloof from the sufferings of his children. Rather, he has a God who, in wonderful ways, takes the *minus* of our sufferings and, if we will but let him, makes them into a *plus.*

Let me give you one illustration of this. Paul, in a wonderful passage in one of his letters (II Corinthians 12), lifts the veil of his privacy and tells us about a period of suffering in his own life and what he made of it all. Things had been going extraordinarily well with him. It was not just that he had been a successful man as the world counts success. No; he had been through a period of spiritual enlightenment and excitement, his contact with God had seemed close and vivid. Then it struck! Exactly what "it" was is not totally clear; he describes it as a stake, or thorn, in the flesh—probably some form of sharp physical pain which "bruised" him. What was he to do? He did what any Christian disciple would naturally do. He asked the Lord to rid him of it. And he kept at it, praying his prayer not once nor twice but thrice. God answered his prayer—with a clear no. Why? The reason is not explicitly given. But the result is clearly seen. *Through* that suffering, Paul was to learn something which he could not learn *without* it. Through it he learned the meaning of God's grace, the power of Christ coming to its full strength in his own weakness, and the overshadowing nearness of Christ himself. That was worth all the suffering. It always is.

When I was a teacher of theological students, I used to tell them that there is a "Christian theology of prepositions." You remember what prepositions are—those little words like "out of" and "through" and "in," and so on? I believe that God's favorite preposition is not "out of" but "in" or "through." "When thou passest *through* the waters, I will be with thee." *"In* the midst of the fire, . . . the fourth like the Son of God." "Most gladly therefore will I . . . glory *in* my infirmities, that the power of Christ may rest upon me."

11. Anxiety

I want to talk to you now about the subject of *anxiety*. I do so because I believe it is a problem to very many people, and clearly more so to some than to others. It is partly a matter of temperament. Some people seem to be so constituted that worry very rarely affects them—they whistle their way through life! Of course, sometimes they whistle just to keep their courage up, and the whistling is a kind of bravado. But there can be little doubt that some people are so constitutionally made that they see the bright side of life, minimize the cloud effects, and live a day at a time with scarcely a glance at the possibilities of ill that may be lurking ahead.

On the other hand, there are those who are as prone to the assaults of anxiety as others are to accidents! The possibility of disaster around the corner, the failure to enjoy the present because of what the future may hold, anxiety about their relatives and friends, not to mention themselves—these are realities to them which the more light-hearted should never underestimate and certainly never laugh at. These anxiety-prone people live in a world of shadows rather than of sunshine. We should feel for them and try to understand them.

Anxiety and depression are close cousins. Medicine can sometimes help, and the use of modern drugs, prescribed by a really skilled doctor, will often lift the clouds. Sheer tiredness and exhaustion can make the clouds look far more menacing and lowering than they really are. The effect of the body on the mind and spirit, the years of adolescence and the changes of middle life, so far from being underestimated should be taken into full consideration, and full use should be made of the help which modern medicine has to offer. God is the God of *all* truth. It is his Spirit which has enabled medicine to advance. He is foolish who does not make full use of it.

Notice how the Bible takes full note of the physical part of our makeup. It is not a mark of "spirituality" to neglect or seek to underestimate the importance of the physical. Let me give you an example from the Old Testament. You may recall the story of Elijah's encounter with the prophets of Baal recorded in I Kings 18. It is a terrific scene—the prophet's challenge to four hundred ranting polytheists, and the eventual vindication of monotheistic religion. What a scene! And what a victory! *But* there was an aftermath. Exhaustion physical and nervous set in—small wonder! Poor Elijah! What did the future hold? For all his victory over the false prophets, he was but a poor thing—"no better than my fathers." He had had enough—too much, in fact. Death would be a pleasant way out. "O Lord, take away my life." A typical state of anxiety and depression.

What is the answer to this? What would you have done if you had had to minister to Elijah? If you were foolish, you would have said to him, "Pull yourself together and get on with your work." But that was precisely what he could *not* do—he had no heart for it at that moment. Or you might have said: "What you need is a spiritual retreat or to go to a religious convention. You are a sinner to talk like this! What has happened to your sense of call? Down on your knees and repent!" What did *God* say? According to the record, he prescribed sleep and food! And that not once, but twice. How very earthy and mundane! Yes, but our religion is just that. It has, in all its fullness in Christ, a strong doctrine of creation and incarnation, of a God who rejoices in the beauty of the body, of a God who in the Person of his Son *took flesh,* of a Christ who knew what it was to be famished with hunger and worn out with work. Don't neglect the body and think it is spiritual to do so. It is sub-Christian.

That needs saying and remembering and acting on.

Then we come to the Gospels. Has Jesus anything to say about anxiety? Indeed he has. That is not surprising, for he lived among a people who had every reason to be anxious.

They were a subject people, subject to the Romans. They were heavily taxed. They had very few medical facilities and little or no state aid in the sense in which we understand that term. There was plenty of cause for anxiety. What has Jesus to say?

It is clear that he treated the matter with the utmost seriousness. He would not mock the people by saying, "Don't worry; it may never happen." He would go deeper than that, because he cared deeply for those to whom he spoke.

What does he say? According to the old Authorized Version in the Sermon on the Mount, he said: "Take no thought for the morrow; take no thought about what ye shall eat or what ye shall drink." But clearly *that* would be to court disaster. Think of the mother who followed that advice as Christmas drew near and the family was gathering, or as the children's clothes and shoes began to wear out! No, Jesus never taught reckless improvidence. What he *did* say was: "Do not be anxious about . . . " "Put away anxious thought about . . . what you have to eat, or what you have to drink.

The passage in which this matter is elaborated —it comes in Matthew 6—seems to me to say two things which are distinctly helpful. *First,* it says in effect: "Get your priorities right. Get your mind working on the great subjects of God's reign and of his justice, of life itself and what it means to live fully as God intends us to live; get busy on *that,* and a sense of balance will be restored to you, a sense of proportion." I think that this is a word which we need to hear and heed in an age which is madly materialistic. Look at the advertisements on your television screen and listen to the people who put them across. You might imagine that it was a matter of life and death whether you bought the very latest thing in washing machines or in soap powder. Or look at the people who line up to get a bargain in the sales after Christmas and almost fight lest they be deprived of a cheap mink coat! These are not people who, like the millions in India and Latin America, do not know where their next meal is coming from. Their pockets are well lined, and their bank balances are considerable. But the greed bug has got them. Their priorities are all upside down. They would do well to listen to this word from the Sermon on the Mount. They might conceivably save themselves from a thrombosis or an ulcer.

Secondly, this passage from the Sermon on the Mount, in the context of the subject of anxiety, keeps talking about "your heavenly *Father.*" Is there a clue here to the alleviation, or even the cure, of anxiety? I think so—certainly if you take this teaching about the Fatherhood of God seriously.

Clearly Jesus, when he spoke of God as Father, thought in terms of a father who cares for and provides for and can be trusted by his children. Not all fathers are like that, by any means. There are fathers whose children are battered and neglected and frightened—and that is what the word "father" connotes to them. But the reverse of this was in the mind of Jesus. Perhaps the kind of caring father that he had in mind was, incidentally, a tribute to Joseph who stood in that kind of relationship to him.

What Jesus is saying is something like this: "A little child in the dark is not frightened if his hand is firmly in the grasp of his father's. The child is confident that the father knows the way out of the darkness into the light, out of danger into security. He cares. He will provide. He can be trusted."

Again, when Jesus speaks of the reign of God and teaches us to think of God as King, he is saying to us in effect: "God has not abdicated. He reigns. He is in control, however black the circumstances may look. His kingdom will come, and you have a share in its coming."

If we turn from Matthew's Gospel to John's, we find a similar emphasis in the teaching of Jesus, though in a very different context. Here, in the fourteenth chapter of John, we hear Jesus saying: "Let not your hearts be troubled," or, as the New English Bible puts it: "Set your troubled hearts at rest." The context in which this passage occurs is significant: Judas is about to betray Jesus. Peter is bragging that he will never defect. The shadow of the Cross is athwart the path of Jesus. In *that* context Jesus says to his friends: "No need to be harassed. Set your troubled hearts at rest." How *can* he say this—and at such a time? The answer is clear. "You believe in God; you are to believe in me too." *Now we see the reason why Jesus takes anxiety so seriously. It is because anxiety is the opposite of trust, of faith in the living God.*

What is faith? It is the transference of trust in myself to trust in the totally reliable God as revealed to us in Christ. When that tranference takes place, the clouds of anxiety begin to disperse, and the sun begins to shine through.

A German hymn writer has put it well:

> All my hope on God is founded;
>   He doth still my trust renew.
> Me through change and chance he guideth,
>   Only good and only true.
>   God unknown,
>   He alone
>   Calls my heart to be his own.
>
> Pride of man and earthly glory,
>   Sword and crown betray his trust;
> What with care and toil he buildeth,
>   Tower and temple, fall to dust.
>   But God's power,
>   Hour by hour,
>   Is my temple and my tower.
>   (Robert Bridges)

This does not mean that there are no storms ahead for the Christian. He who said "Let not your hearts be storm-tossed" found himself storm-tossed in the agony of Gethsemane. The ocean waves sometimes beat high, but underneath there is the great calm of the great deep.

Paul got it right. "The Lord is near," he wrote. "Have no anxiety, but in everything make your requests known to God in prayer and petition with thanksgiving. Then the peace of God, which is beyond our utmost understanding, will keep guard over your hearts and your thoughts, in Christ Jesus" (NEB).

12. Discipleship

A disciple, says the Oxford English Dictionary, is "one who attends upon another for the purpose of learning from him; a pupil or scholar." It is a good definition. It implies a long process of learning—the pupil *"attends upon"* the teacher. And the main point of the definition is *learning.*

The aspect of relationship is, of course, of great importance. The inner circle of the little band of Jesus' disciples rubbed shoulders with him constantly. And when his physical presence was withdrawn and they could see and feel him no more, they still continued in a close relationship with him. They spoke with him in the fellowship of his church and in the intimacy of their private prayers. To them, he was not the memory of one to whom they nostalgically looked back. On the contrary, he was a companion, unseen but loved, with whom they constantly conversed.

Yes, *constantly.* For, as we have said, discipleship implies a long process of learning. When, today, we say that Smith is a disciple of Marx or Freud or Beethoven, we mean that, over a long period, Smith has so studied their works and examined their tenets as to be convinced that they are in the right in their particular field. Others in that field may have a good deal to be said for them; but so far as Smith can see, the man to whose school he belongs has something the others haven't got. He has drunk deep at that particular well and is satisfied as he can be nowhere else. He is content to be a disciple of Marx or Freud or Beethoven or whoever.

And *learning*—that is at the very heart of being a disciple. There is a wonderful passage in Matthew's Gospel (11:28-30) in which the Evangelist reports Jesus as saying: "Come to me, all whose work is hard, whose load is heavy; and I will give you relief. Bend your necks to my yoke, and learn from me, for I am gentle and humble-hearted; and your souls will find relief. For my yoke is good to bear, my load is light" (NEB). If you imagine the setting in which those words were said, you can appreciate how apposite they were. The Jews of our Lord's day were a subject nation, subject to the Roman yoke. It was not an easy yoke. It hurt them and galled them. Taxation was high. Hours of work were long. Conditions were bad. They would have given anything to be free of it. Here was one who promised them relief—not indeed from Roman domination (for he refused to act as a political or military deliverer), but from the burden of bitterness, hatred, and sin which broke a man's spirit.

The terms of his invitation are extremely

interesting. He offers them another yoke! But to bend their necks to that would surely be to escape from one bondage into another? Not at all. The Roman yoke was imposed by force; they had no option but to endure it. They must carry it alone—there was no one to help them. But Christ's yoke is not imposed by force. To bend their necks to that yoke is by invitation, and they are free to do as they will. If they do decide to accept the invitation and bend their necks to his yoke, they will find that it is a shared yoke and that he who invites them carries the greater part of the load.

"My yoke is good to bear, my load is light." Was this the wording of the advertisement over the Galilean carpenter's shop? It might well have been. We may be sure that no rough yoke which would have irked the neck of the cattle ever went out from that little factory. Jesus took good care of that. So it is with the yoke of Christian discipleship. What might have been thought to be bondage turns out to be freedom. What might have been conceived of as restrictive is found to be liberating. Here is the supreme paradox of discipleship in a nutshell.

Perhaps it is because "discipline" is a cousin-word to "discipleship" that we think of the latter with a touch of grimness. There is nothing grim about being a disciple of Jesus! There is freedom and laughter and joy. But there is the tougher side as well. Discipleship *does* involve discipline, and discipline is tough. This is a very real ingredient in New Testament teaching about being a follower of Jesus, about belonging to his school. Self-control is an authentic part of the harvest of the Spirit to which Paul refers in his Letter to the Galatians. Endurance is a major part of the Christian ethic—the sheer power to stick it through when practically everybody is against you and when you represent the Spirit of Christ in an age which largely rejects that Spirit. The readiness to undergo suffering, the suffering which chastens and toughens and makes character—that, too, is part of Christian discipline; as is the readiness to say, "No, I can wait," rather than, "Give it to me now; I must grab it."

Stewardship is part of Christian discipleship and discipline. By stewardship I mean a down-to-earth recognition that I own nothing—I am lent a great deal by a lavish God, and therefore I am responsible for what use I make of the loan. The *time* I am given is a loan to me from God. I must not fritter it away. Opportunities must be bought up—they may not present themselves again. *Talents* must be put to the best possible use. And the *money* which I have by earning or by inheritance is a trust for which I shall have to give an account. Stewardship, therefore, is not a bright idea thought up by those who want to make money to repair the church roof or to add another console to the church organ. It is a constituent part of Christian discipleship, the logical outcome of acknowledging Christ's lordship. It is part and parcel of Christian responsibility, of my response to the Christ who loved me and gave himself up for me.

When Jesus first called the two pairs of brothers, Simon and Andrew, and James and John, to be his disciples, it is said that they, in the first case, left their nets, and, in the second, they left the boat and their father. This has often proved to be part of Christian discipleship—and a very costly part. There has to be a break if obedience is to be complete. *Then* they "followed him." I like that phrase. I can see him striding on ahead; I can see them stumbling on and trying to keep up! But there were his footprints into which they could plant their own feet—and that made all the difference. That is the way of discipleship—Jesus is never far off, always marking out the way, always challenging us with a divine discontent and pointing the way ahead to the heights which we had not even glimpsed before. Pretty strenuous—but oh, how exciting!

I want to go back for a moment to that dictionary definition of a disciple: "one who attends upon another for the purpose of learning from him; a pupil or scholar." From one point of view, that definition of a disciple includes within it a good definition of *prayer* —"one attending upon another for the purpose of learning from him." Prayer is the most vital part of the discipline of a disciple. In fact, discipleship withers if prayer goes by default. For friendships must be kept in repair; and discipleship, after all, is friendship. In prayer, the learner "attends upon" the Teacher—"what have you to teach me today?" The immature mind attends upon him who "is made unto us wisdom." The slave attends upon the Master—"what are your orders for me today?" The son communes with the Father in a relationship of ever-increasing depth. Prayer is the vital breath of discipleship.

How can we test whether in fact we are in any real and living sense disciples of Jesus? There are many tests. Let me mention but two.

The first is a very practical one—the test of *love*. "By this shall all men know that ye are my disciples, if ye have love one to another" (John 13:35). The context of this passage is that of the Christian community. It should be possible, in any given area, to detect the Christian community by the sheer quality, the depth, the warmth, of the love which the members of the Christian church have toward one another. How urgent does this test make our ecumenical relationships! Suspicion and ignorance of one another have to go, and their place must be taken by a loving understanding and caring. Here is a test—perhaps the supreme test—for the integrity of your own church—that its members love one another. It's as simple and straightforward and down to earth as that! And let me remind you, in this context, that love is no soft sentimentality, but the rigorous "set of the will for the eternal welfare of another."

The second test is *fruit-bearing.* "This is my Father's glory, that you may bear fruit in plenty and so be my disciples" (NEB). What is the fruit referred to here? Your guess is as good as mine. I think it means sheer obedience. "You are my friends, *if* you do what I command you." Disobedience means no fruit-bearing. Obedience in the little things—the suggestions of conscience, the orders that come to you while you are praying—this is what matters. When we live a life of obedience in these little things, obedience in the big things, when the crises of decisions come, is more likely to follow.

"Fruit-bearing" ultimately, I suppose, is the growing of a Christian character, a personality like that of Jesus. And that, to end where we began, means "attending" on him for the purpose of learning from him.

13. Guidance

One of the things which puzzles people today—at least those who take religion at all seriously—is the subject of guidance. *Is* there such a thing? Does God guide his children? Or do they have to trudge along as best they can and just hope that they are going in the right direction?

To some of us—let's be honest—it seems almost annoying that some people appear to be so sure about guidance. It would be unkind to say they are cocky about it! But they seem to have a direct line to God, and their guidance comes through without interference! Most of us do *not* find things work out like this. Guidance for us is a much more complicated business. Indeed there are those—and among them very real Chrisitian disciples—who seem much more often in the dark than in the light. Or, to change the metaphor, God seems to them much more often to keep silent than to speak a word of direction or guidance. And this makes being a disciple pretty difficult.

Let's have a look at this and see if we can make any sense of it all. We'll begin by having a look at what God is like. We must go to the teaching of

Jesus for this. He liked to speak of God mostly as *Father.* To him that presumably conjured up a figure who loved and cared for his children. Their good was his great concern—their eternal welfare. That might—indeed would—include discipline. But surely, also, it would include guidance. A father who did not seek to guide his children would scarcely deserve the name of father.

Jesus also spoke of God as *King.* He would be a strange king who did not constantly seek ways and means of disclosing his will to his people. The British sovereign broadcasts regularly to her peoples all over the world. The President of the United States gives his talks, formal and informal, to the nation.

So, if Jesus was right in speaking to us of God as Father and King, we must infer that part of that relationship will be found in the guiding of his children, the directing of his people. That we should expect.

Within a family circle, guidance takes different shapes at the different stages of the child's development. When the child is small, guidance has necessarily to come in the form of oft-repeated, specific directions: "Shut the door quietly. Wash your hands. Don't play with fire. Read more slowly and carefully." But when the child reaches adolescence, such specific directions are no longer necessary. Those lessons have been learned and are now part of him. And when the adolescent has become fully adult, direction from father or mother takes an almost wholly different form. It is more the interplay of a mature mind on a less fully matured one. It is the sharing of wisdom with one less deeply experienced. It is still needed, but the form of the guidance has changed from that of earlier years.

I think this is true also in Christian experience. To many who have recently come to know, love, and serve God, there is a clarity about their guidance which is almost luminous. The Bible seems to hold all the answers to their immediate needs. Indeed, what some rather irreverently call the lucky-dip method seems to work for them—open your Bible, put your finger on any verse, and—presto—there is guidance for you. Quite frankly, I don't find that method works for me, and I don't particularly want it to! But I have no doubt that there are many who would say it has worked for them, and who am I to deny it?

To most Christians, however, guidance is not such a luminously clear and direct affair. To many, there are clouds and difficulties in the way, yes, and doubt too. Is it possible that God is treating them not as children but as adolescents in the Christian way, or even as adults? Is the absence of quick and easy guidance a sign of his trust in us? Is it a testing and thereby a strengthening of faith and endurance? Maybe. If so, it's worth working away at the subject.

What are the requisites for the obtaining of

guidance from God? Or, to put it better perhaps, what aids are there?

Quite clearly, the fundamental requisite is a desire on our part to know God, to know his will, and a readiness to do it. It is *our* will, our willingness, that matters. The psalmists knew a lot about this. One of them saw the uselessness, the ineffectiveness, of animal sacrifice, and told God about it. Then he went on: "Then said I, Lo, I come. . . . I delight to do thy will, O my God: yea, thy law is within my heart." That is getting pretty close to the nub of the matter. "Teach me to do thy will, O my God," another psalmist cried with a kind of passion in his heart. "My soul thirsteth for God, for the living God," said a third. That is the kind of setting of the will Godward which makes possible the revelation of God's will manward.

Then the next requisite, the next aid, is prayer—prayer not so much in terms of asking God for things, as waiting on God. "My soul doth *wait* for him," said the psalmist. Perhaps that is the most fruitful form of communion with God—and the hardest for us fussy, hurried activists! When two people grow old together, they often reach the point of closeness where it is enough for them just to *be* together for the most satisfying fellowship to take place. Little or no conversation is necessary. They are in each other's presence, and in that they find their deepest satisfaction. Is that what the psalmist meant when he wrote about waiting for God?

Might *that* be the best setting for receiving the guidance of God?

How slow we are in abandoning the view that prayer is primarily asking God for things. I am not saying that this is not part of prayer—Jesus seems to have taught us that there was a place for this. In the Lord's Prayer, he encouraged us to ask for daily bread, for forgiveness, for delivery from evil, though even these requests were prefaced by prayers which sought for the hallowing of God's name, the coming of his reign, the doing of his will. No, there is a place for asking, but it is not the *primary* activity of prayer. Prayer is more seeking—"What is your will, Father? What do you want me to do? Or to be? Or to undertake? Or to try to understand?" Adoration has its important part. So have praise and thanksgiving—they open up the springs of joy in our hearts. To ponder on the magnificence of God widens our horizons and cures our pettiness. To engage in intercession for others delivers us from self-centeredness and any tendency to self-pity. Prayer is a health-giving exercise and makes the revelation of God's guidance more possible. It disperses the fog and allows the sunshine to get through.

Then what about the Bible? This, I am sure, has a very important part to play in this business of guidance. The "devotional use" of the Bible is a phrase which has been badly misused in the past. It has sometimes meant the abandonment of an intelligent approach to the Scriptures and a kind of warm and cozy sentimentality of approach which does harm to the mind. This is not the way to approach the Bible. We need to use all the brains we have and to put them at the disposal of the Illuminator Spirit. "Thou shalt love the Lord thy God with all they mind" has a direct bearing on our work on the Bible. We must not wrench passages out of their context. We must take full cognizance of the conditions in which the books were written and of the limitations under which the writers suffered. We do not worship the Bible—we are not bibliolators. We worship the Lord of the Bible. But we remember what Martin Luther used to say—that the Bible is the cradle in which Jesus is borne to us, and we treat it with the reverence due to it. For centuries it has carried the Christ to men and women of all kinds—to scholars and to the ignorant, to rich and poor, to prince and peasant. It could carry him to us.

Therefore, we preface our Bible study with prayer, that the Spirit may take of it and show us the truth—each day a little bit more fully; show us the principles on which God has dealt with his people, and deals with them still; show us the wonder of Christ, of his church, of his patience. And at the end of our study we turn it into a prayer—that what has been disclosed may be incorporated in holier living and more vigorous discipleship.

In what I have said, I have assumed some regularity in our Bible reading—the use of some simple scheme by which we read not just our favorite sections picked out almost at random, but a scheme by which, over a period, we can begin to grasp the outline of God's way with his people, the principles on which he works with them, and the kind of characters he wants to build in them. Such reading, seasoned with prayer, allows the light in and the guidance to come through.

There is another aid in the finding of God's guidance that I must mention. By myself, alone, I have very little wisdom. I am very fallible. My own desires can so easily be mistaken for God's will. I need at once those who will help me check my fallible judgment and at the same time put their wisdom and experience at my disposal. In short, I need the advice of friends. That is why God in his wisdom has given me the fellowship of the church. He never intended me to be a solitary disciple, divorced from the loving guidance of others who, in all probability, are living closer to God than I am and are more receptive to his instructions. The wisdom of the ages is not to be found in me, nor ever will be. But in my fellow members in the Body of Christ there is a great deal of it, and in the rich biographies of those who have gone on ahead there is more of it. Why should I impoverish myself by refraining from drawing on such a bank?

I have made four points. I could make more, but these will suffice. I have said, in short, that these are the aids which will help me in finding God's guidance: a desire and readiness to do God's will; prayer; the Bible; the help of Christian friends. At the place where these four points meet, you won't be very far from the place of God's will. If, on the other hand, you come to your seeking with an unwilling heart; if your prayer is formal and peremptory; if the principles of the biblical revelation are contrary to what you have in mind; if experinced friends are unanimous in advising you against it, then it is probably the case that you had best wait and ask again. It looks as if the light is red.

Let me close with a word of warning. God, for reasons best known to him, doesn't seem to favor giving blueprints, maps of the distant future. On the contrary, he seems to tell us to go a step at a time and trust him for the rest. I suppose that is what is meant by the walk of faith—not a key to unlock the future, but a torch to light up the path, a path wide enough for two, for him and you to walk together.

So, though there will occasionally be big life-decisions on which you will need his guidance, generally it will be day-by-day direction that you'll have need to find. And that means step-by-step dependence on his grace and strength, and step-by-step obedience.

And that's the happy way to live.

14. Prayer

Faith and prayer go together. Earlier I spoke of faith as "a very personal relationship between a man and God in Christ; the transference of trust from fallible, sinful self to the totally reliable God." So much for *faith*. But what about *prayer?*

This also is an intensely personal thing—a meeting of the finite with the infinite. When the man of faith presses his littleness close to God's greatness in prayer, his ignorance close to God's wisdom, his weakness close to God's strength, yes, and (greatly daring) his sinfulness close to God's holy forgiving, it is personal indeed. But faith is like that—personal contact with God, beginning in so small a way but having within it the potentiality of almost infinite growth.

But to leave it there would be to truncate the true meaning of prayer. For if prayer, like faith, is a deeply personal thing, it is also, again like faith, a fundamentally corporate thing. If faith functions in the setting of "all God's people," so does prayer.

I believe that it is because we fail to realize this that we become so discouraged in our praying and so despondent about it that we either relapse into mere formality or give it up altogether. God is so great; the universe is so huge and so mysterious; life, suffering, death are so far beyond our comprehension. What is the point of our feeble little attempts at prayer, the broadcasts of tiny individuals in a great echoing vastness?

There are at least three errors in such an argument. The first is that prayer is our broadcast to the Almighty. It is not. It is our communion with him and his with us.

The second is that it fails to appreciate that, at the center of the "great echoing vastness," beats the heart of a loving God. Jesus dared to speak of that God in terms of fatherhood and kingship, that is to say, of love and authority. Marry those two concepts and you will begin to see what God is like. Was it C. S. Lewis who used to warn us not to think of God as a great managing director who could not be bothered with the newest little office boy? God's fatherly care reaches to the least significant, for "significance" is a human term which has no significance for the heavenly Father!

The third error in the argument is that it overindividualizes prayer. It fails to perceive its essentially corporate nature. When I pray, it is not one little piper piping alone. It is certainly one individual, but *joining in an orchestra.*

The whole church of God makes up that orchestra. It has been playing ever since there was a church. It began at least as long ago as Abraham. It took on a new dimension when those two pairs of brothers made their response by the Lake of Galilee. It gained a fresh jubilation at Pentecost. Now its members come from all over the world, and the greater part of them have gone on ahead. But it is one orchestra. It is unlimited by space or time; it transcends both. It goes on—and will go on till the Great Day. And then all its disharmonies will fade away. Meanwhile, when I pray—even when I am at my coldest and most formal—I join in; I take my part in the great orchestra; I am one with angels and archangels and all the company of heaven. That helps me to get my perspectives of prayer right.

Prayer is then at once an intensely individual activity and it is a corporate activity. It is the response of the beloved to the great Lover, of the child to the Father. But it is more. It is the response of the subject to the King—for Jesus, when he spoke of God, did so in terms not only of fatherhood but also of kingship. The reign of God seems to have been the dominant theme of his teaching. We must pause here.

When I come before God in prayer, I come as a subject who would learn the meaning and the implications of that relationship. Really to pray is to stand at attention in the presence of the King and to be prepared to take orders from him. It is to concentrate into these few moments what should increasingly be the whole attitude of my life—namely, obedience to the will of God, in things great and small, as he sees fit to make that will known.

When Jesus prayed "thy kingdom come, thy will be done"; when, near the end of his earthly life, he prayed "Not my will, but thine be done," he focused into those few words a *life-attitude*. It is likely that *he* attained that attitude and so was able to pray those prayers, not without difficulty. He *learned* obedience, and learned it through suffering (Hebrews 5:8).

To "delight to do thy will" and to do it "with my whole heart" is not likely to come easily to us self-centered sinners, for the sinless Son of man had his struggles! Hence the need for those oft-repeated moments of will-focusing which, increasingly over the years, will merge into a life-attitude. The saints would appear to tell us that the *only* prayer that matters is "Thy will be done." To pray that prayer perfectly, to align my little will with the "good, acceptable and perfect" will of God—that is the end greatly to be desired. That is the goal of discipleship. Then the prayer "Thy will be done" is not uttered in a minor tone as a kind of recognition of the inevitable, but as a triumph-cry—this is the best that can happen to anyone living!

Luke records a remarkable word of Jesus which none of the other Evangelists mentions. The New English Bible renders it "You are the men who have stood firmly by me in my times of trial" (22:28). The setting of the saying is a somber one. The Eucharist had been instituted. Jesus has told his friends that, in the little group around the table, there is one who will betray

him. Then—of all times and places!—a dispute
breaks out as to which of them should rank
highest, and Jesus has to give them an object
lesson in the meaning of service. Against that
dismal background, he pays his men a glorious
tribute: "You are the men who have stood firmly
by me in my times of trial." They had been with
him when the crowds in their thousands hung
upon his words. That was easy. But, when the
crowds disappeared and the numbers who
followed him were small, when the people grew
suspicious and their leaders violently opposed
him, still those men stood firmly by him. That
was hard. And it was splendid.

The worst lay ahead, and Jesus was quick to
warn them. "Satan has been given leave to sift all
of you like wheat" (NEB). "Hosanna" is to give
place to "Crucify," and that within hours. "But
Simon, Simon, I have concentrated my prayer
on *you*"(the plural has given way to the singular)
"that your faith may not fail." After all, he was to
be the leader. He had singular gifts in that
direction—and singular weaknesses too! The
great test was around the corner—and with the
test, dismal defeat.   Talk about unanswered
prayer! "I have prayed for you"—and Simon
squirmed under the sneer of a servant girl and
denied his Lord thrice. Unanswered prayer?
Yes, and no. Immediately unanswered, yes. In
the longer view, wonderfully answered. The
prayer was "that your *faith* may not fail." A
relationship had been established between

Jesus and Simon Peter, a relationship of a most intimate and personal kind. It was to undergo the most fearful stress. From Peter's side it was to be strained to breaking point, but not from the side of Jesus. Though Peter was unfaithful, Christ was not. After the cross and resurrection came renewal and recommissioning and, at Pentecost, re-empowering. The faith relationship, established by the Lake of Galilee, strengthened in those times of trial, did not finally break. On the contrary, over the next thirty years and more, it was to grow infinitely stronger, more resilient, more deep. Like his friend Paul, Peter was to be "in journeyings oft" and, according to the stories in the Acts, he was to experience the testing fires. If (as there is good evidence to believe) the First Epistle of Peter comes from his hand, it reflects a situation of severe testing, but it reflects also a "faith which has stood the test" and "a joy too great for words" (I Peter 1:7-8 NEB).

We need not doubt that the exhortation (in I Peter 4:7) to a life "given to prayer" sprang out of his own experience of just such a life lived down the long years. The relationship of faith was nourished by the life of prayer, and in the process acquired a depth which Peter could never have imagined back in the Galilean days.

The last thirty-odd years, the years since the end of the Second World War, have been "times of trial" for Christ's church. While the church has made immense strides in Africa and Latin

America, in Britain and in North America the
winds have been blowing fierce and cold.
Active, practicing Christians have been seen for
the minority that they are. Many have lost their
faith in any positive proclamation of a gospel
rooted in the historic facts of God's revelation in
Christ, and have reached the point where they
feel that they can only engage in activities of a
social nature as expressing generally accepted
Christian principles. They can do little more than
ask questions; they cannot "declare." Others
have become so absorbed in restructuring the
church that their vision of what the church really
is has become clouded. Others, again, have so
concentrated their energies on such subjects as
ecumenism or liturgical revision as to give the
impression that these are ends in themselves.
The best has been submerged by the good. The
fires of a personal devotion to our Lord have
burned low. Prayer has become formal; indeed,
many have questioned whether prayer, in the
sense that the church has understood it down
the long centuries, will avail for "man come of
age."

Perhaps two things are called for in these
times of trial. The first is just that endurance for
which, so Luke tells us, Jesus commended his
followers. To some, endurance would seem to
be a very humdrum virtue. But in the New
Testament it is one of the most highly commended. The grace to stick it through when
others defect; the power to hold to the

essentials when others concentrate on the peripheral; the ability to face, undiscouraged, the implications of belonging to a minority movement, in fact to endure—and endure joyfully—the shame of the Cross—all this, in part, is the meaning of Christian endurance.

This is a very unspectacular virtue, but it is one of fundamental importance. It is commended of our Lord to be honorable among his followers. I can conceive of no higher honor than that, at the end of the journey, he should say of me and my fellow Christians: "You are the men, and women, who have stood firmly by me in my times of trial." The relationship of faith, at once so intimately personal and so powerfully corporate, has been deepened by the life of prayer —and it has stood the test.

The second thing that is called for in these times of trial is a new grasp of the meaning of *hope.* After all, hope is faith-looking-forward. Hope is confidence in the God who is not only the God of Abraham, Isaac, and Jacob, but the God "who *will become* what he will become," the God not only of the historic past, but of the future.

Men of faith, who are necessarily also men of hope, know that God has not abdicated. He is the God of surprises. "The best is yet to be" precisely because "best of all, God is with us."

All this has an immediate bearing on prayer. The Christian, in entering into a faith relationship with God in Christ, has by the same token entered into a hope relationship with that God. It follows, then, that when, in prayer, he approaches God, he does so in a "waiting attitude of expectation," in a stance of questioning. Study the Psalms, that prayerbook of the ancient Jewish church, and you will see how many of the prayers are in the form of questions put by the petitioner to God. This is not quite the same as the point made earlier, that prayer is standing at attention in the presence of God and awaiting his orders. This, rather, is coming into the presence of God with the question posed: "What surprises have you got today, Lord? For you are the God of the new, the hitherto unrevealed, the unexpected."

After all, outside the room where a Christian is praying, the appropriate notice is not so much "Quiet! Christian at prayer," as "Look out! *God* at work!"

15. Bible

The Bible is a dated book, or, more accurately, a little library of dated books. How could it be otherwise? The most recent of the books was written nearly nineteen hundred years ago; the most ancient, many centuries earlier than that. It tells, in picture language, of the beginning of things, of primitive times and ancient love stories, of battles long ago. It is a strange mixture of poetry and prose, of parables and letters, of prophecy and history.

Can the Bible still be a way in which God comes through to us in power and love? The Eucharist? Yes. Prayer? Yes. But the Bible?

The fact is that it has proved just that—a means of grace—to men and women of all kinds down the long centuries, and still is just that to millions today. This is in spite of modern man's having "come of age," as that much-quoted phrase goes; in spite of his being a highly sophisticated, scientifically oriented creature, so very different in many ways from those who wrote the Bible and from those for whom it was originally intended.

What is the explanation of this undoubted fact?

It lies, I think, partly in this—that the Bible is very largely a book of biography. It consists of life-stories of men and women looked at as individuals and as members of communities.

While it is true that we humans change from century to century in many respects—men who lived before the discovery of the wheel were very different from those, like ourselves, who live in the space age—yet, beneath these surface differences lie certain characteristics which do not change from millennium to millennium—our need for love, for forgiveness, for happy community relations, for light on the basic problems of human existence and on life after death, and so on.

Another reason why this ancient book, dated as it undoubtedly is, seems to transcend the centuries and becomes a means of grace to modern man is this. It talks about *God.* Indeed this is the main burden of its message. From one point of view, it is the story of man's search for God—and there are parts of that search-story which, in the full light of the Christian revelation, do not prove very edifying or enlightening. But, from a much more important angle, the Bible can be viewed as the agelong story of God's search for man: "Adam, where art thou?" *Here* lies the permanent value of the Bible, for Christians believe that God is still on the search for man, and that his great heart of love is not satisfied till man comes to himself and comes to his Father, and so finds his rest in God.

The Bible is a book that speaks to men of different ages and backgrounds. Perhaps we should more accurately say, the Bible is a book through which, as through no other book, the Spirit of the living God speaks to men, under the widely varying conditions in which they find themselves. Coleridge used to say that it has a way of "finding" the devout reader of its pages. That is not a bad way of putting it.

So, in developing our theme, we shall take different circumstances in which man finds himself and in which the Bible has a relevant word to speak.

If I frequently illustrate what I have to say from human experience, that will not be surprising, for the simple reason that we have already noted, that the Bible is full of biographical material.

First of all, *in times of crisis,* how often we need guidance! Has the Bible anything to say about how to get it? I think it has. I look at two people who have something to say on the matter.

The first was a king who lived in the Near East in the eighth century before Christ. His nation was a small one; his temporal power was not very great. Power lay in the hands of the great nations which lay to the north and east of his land of Israel—nations like Assyria. It was from Assyria that he received one day a letter couched in terms that would make any king tremble for the safety of his people and his throne. It was a mocking letter: "Don't start bragging about the power of your God to deliver you from my hand! Look at the other nations which I have subdued, and what has happened to them! Of what avail were their prayers to their gods? You had better learn your lesson—and submit, before I crush you."

It was a terrible ultimatum. Great issues were at stake. How Hezekiah needed the guidance of God!

This is what he did. He took the letter from the hand of the messengers who had brought it. He read it. He went up to the temple of the Lord and spread it out before the Lord, and poured his heart out in prayer.

The details of how God answered that prayer through the prophet Isaiah need not concern us now. But the action of Hezekiah certainly has a lesson if we are trying to see how God guides on important occasions.

It would have been possible for him to rush into battle in a fury at the cheek of the king of Assyria. It would have been possible for him to submit, or to flee from his post of responsibility. He did neither of these things. Quietly he laid the matter before God—and waited.

He did not wait in vain. No rush, no panic, but prayer. That is how the guidance came.

The second person who learned the way of divine guidance was Jesus Christ himself. There are indications in the Gospels that, before he made great decisions, he would withdraw from the bustle of the town and from the pressure of the crowds, and wait on God in the quiet of the country. He did this, for example, before he chose his twelve closest followers, the apostles. So much hung on this decision. He would not rush into it. He must seek the mind of his Father—unhurriedly. He must ask him for his guidance in the intimacy of dialogue—prayer. These men were to be the leaders of his mission in the months and years ahead. "Father, show me your mind."

As we read between the lines of the Gospels, we see a kind of rhythm in the life of Jesus. Nature has its rhythms of sleeping and waking, the rhythm of withdrawal and activity. So it seems to have been in the life of Jesus, planned with a kind of magisterial serenity—activity preceded by prayer; preaching, healing, teaching following quiet communion with his Father.

It was in this way, I believe, that Jesus may well have come to rely less and less on sudden revelations of guidance from God in times of emergency. By constantly repeated acts of communion with God, he had learned the principles on which he runs his world and seeks to guide his children.

When the crisis came, he knew the way he must go.

Next, *in times of celebration,* we need the Bible. There is a strange idea about that the Bible is a somber book. In the old days it used to be bound in black and printed in small type, and that helped to convey this impression of gloom.

Of course, it does deal with the serious side of human experience—with sin and disease and death, with temptation and doubt and darkness. It would not be a very realistic book if it had not much to say on these things. But, has it anything to say to those for whom life is *good?* Can it be a means of grace at a time of joy and celebration?

The answer most certainly is yes, it can.

The central rite of Christian worship is the Eucharist. The word simply means "thanksgiving." When the church "does this in remembrance" of its crucified and risen Lord, it engages in a celebration, a joyful feast. It uses wine—the symbol of gladness and warmth and cheer. Though that wine speaks of the blood of Christ outpoured in sacrificial giving, it also speaks of exuberant joy.

The story of the turning of the water into wine at the wedding feast in Cana of Galilee was the writer's way of saying that, when Jesus is present and his will is obeyed, there is festival, there is fun, there is something to sing about, something to celebrate!

There is evidence in the Gospels which leads us to think that Jesus had pondered a great deal on the book of Deuteronomy. Now that certainly isn't the first book which you would turn to if you wanted to understand the Bible and you went to it as a comparative beginner! But it has some very interesting things to say. For instance, if you were to open it at the fourteenth chapter, you would find a passage which might not interest you particularly, all about animals and birds that you may or may not eat—a sort of primitive list of health-food laws. But that passage is followed by one which might be headed: "How to enjoy a celebration." It is a description of a kind of super harvest festival, a grand feast, or, if that were to prove impossible, a grand spending spree! No suggestion here that the people of God are spoilsports or dismal imbeciles—people ruled by negatives: "Thou shalt not, thou shalt not, thou shalt not." No, there seems to be a foretaste of what a New Testament writer was later to lay down as a kind of manifesto for positive Christian living: "God has given us richly all things to enjoy."

Here is a life-affirming principle which has not always been followed by the disciples of the One who sometimes seemed more at home, more comfortable, with the worldly types of his day than he did with religious, sour-faced rigorists.

If you look a bit more closely at that passage in Deuteronomy on how to enjoy a celebration, you will find two very interesting things about it. The first is that it is all done "before the Lord." That does not mean that God looks down with a disapproving eye when life is going well with us and we want to celebrate. Not at all. It simply means that we conduct our celebrations, as we seek to conduct all aspects of life (business, leisure, love, the lot), in such a way as he approves, or, to use the accepted religious phrase, "to his glory."

The other thing of interest about this passage is that strict instructions are given not to forget the underprivileged, the people less fortunate than themselves, the socially deprived. The equivalent today would be those who have slipped through the provisions made by the welfare services—and we always have such among us—and, looking further afield, the millions in the third world. While they are around, extravagance is obscene.

The Lord who entered into the joys of the wedding feast and made them infinitely greater by his presence and his action, loves to enter into our celebrations, to share with us when life is good and skies are blue. At the same time he reminds us of those for whom there is little joy in life, little to celebrate about. And he once told a story which illustrated the fact that a man *can* get so obsessed with celebrations, with wealth and all that goes with it, that the seed of eternal life gets choked. That is disaster beyond all telling.

And finally, *in times when the world seems to have gone mad,* we turn to the Bible. Some centuries before Christ was born, a man looked over his world. He had, of course, no radio or television as we have, no newspapers even, to bring that world into his living room and keep him informed from hour to hour of its goings-on. But such news as he got—through passing camel cavalcades, through couriers, through swiftly spreading rumors—convinced him that it was a mad, mad world. The very mountains seemed to shake and, as he put it, the waters seemed to rage and swell. It was like a volcanic eruption. The little land he lived in had proved in past history all too often to be the place over which the great powers fought. His people were a kind of pawn in the unscrupulous hands of competing nations round about! What could a man say? What could he do? Where could he find confidence in a world like *that?*

We do not know the name of the man we have been talking about, but from the poem he wrote we can deduce a good deal about him. He was very much a man of the world. He kept his eyes open and, as we say, he knew a thing or two. But his vision was not confined to what his physical eyes saw about him. He was a man of faith. He had an answer to the question as to where his confidence could be found in a world gone mad. *"God* is our refuge and strength," he said; "a very present help in trouble. Therefore will not we fear, though the earth be removed. . . ." So he kept quiet and listened; and as he listened, strength began to take the place of fear. He heard God speaking: "Be still," he said, "and know that I am God."

Those unknown men who wrote the Psalms breathe a superb confidence through their writings. "God reigns," they say again and again. God has not abdicated, even though men seem to have gone mad. God reigns. God loves. God cares.

Men like them, with their strong note of confidence, can become a means of grace to us who live in even more troubled days than were theirs; days which hold within them possibilities of disaster (nuclear and other) which they never dreamed of, and examples of human folly such as had never occurred to them.

There are many today who are appalled by human insanity and by man's inhumanity to man, and all the more appalled because they feel that they can do so little about it. They do not occupy the seats of power; their word avails little; they seem to be very small cogs in a vast impersonal machine. Perhaps this is especially true of the shut-ins, whose main life-work is behind them; who read the papers and find their stories depressing; who listen in and find the news to be little more than a series of disasters.

To all such people I want to say two things:

First, remember where the psalmist put his trust. Remember that a greater than the psalmist, Jesus Christ himself, dared, in the face of all the terrors of his day, to call God Father and King—a Father who seeks the love of his children; a King who seeks their loyalty and obedience. He dared to hold, in life and in death, that God reigns; that he loves; that he cares.

Secondly, remember that God is not dependent on the big battalions to do his work. He has a way of working through minority groups or even through individuals, undistinguished people, even through men and women who are unconscious of being agents of his power.

That means that *you,* far though you are from what most people conceive of as the corridors of power, that you can be a center of serenity in a world that seems to have gone mad.

If the room where you live becomes a place of prayer, it may be more powerful for good than the council chambers of the nations' potentates.